Merz World: Processing the Complicated Order

Adrian Notz & Hans Ulrich Obrist (eds.)

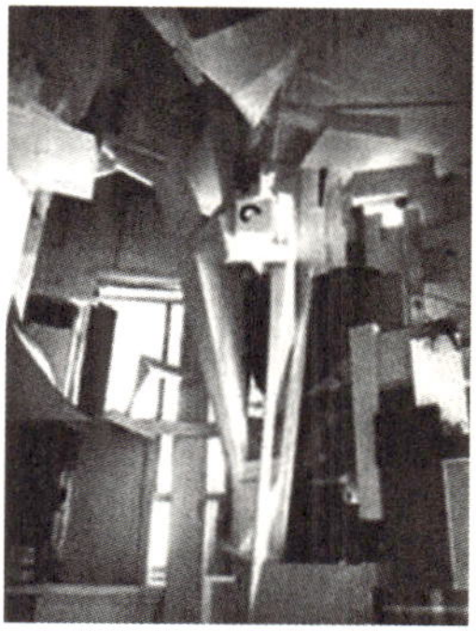

jrp|ringier

Table of Contents

Chapter Two: Processing

This book is dedicated to
the memory of Harald Szeemann.

Preamble

Introduction

Adrian Notz

From 1923 to 1936 the artist Kurt Schwitters (1887–1948) worked on his Merzbau in Hanover, which is said to be the central work in the complete oeuvre of the Merz artist. It was destroyed by an allied air raid in 1943 and only a few photographs and descriptions remain. The Merzbau has therefore been transfigured in many different ways.

Driven by the transfigurations that have befallen the Merzbau, here it will be formulated as a metaphor and module, a device for contemporary artistic, architectural, and social practices and developments. It is used as a trigger for architects and artists to deal with contemporary complexity.

In this publication, scientific insights and historical expertise on the Merzbau are faced with contemporary concepts in architecture, art mediation, and art practice, to open up a new field of research on the Merzbau. This book also links together different texts and discussions on the subject. It is a snapshot of research that has only just begun.

The contributions in this book are extracts from the Symposium Merzbau held on May 7, 2005, at the Cabaret Voltaire in Zurich.

The Merzbau as a Paradigm of Interior Complexity

Hans Ulrich Obrist

To begin at the beginning: any contemporary research into the Merzbau is unthinkable without Harald Szeemann's 1983 exhibition *Der Hang zum Gesamtkunstwerk* (*Tendencies Toward the Total Work of Art*). This was very much an exhibition as a kind of knowledge production. There are many aspects in Szeemann's catalogue text, and also in the notes we find there by Schwitters, that are relevant to a discussion of the Merzbau.

For me, the Merzbau has always been present in the works of many artists throughout the 1990s, and I've had endless discussions with Gabriel Orozco and Rirkrit Tiravanija on Schwitters and the Merzbau. In the latter half of the 1990s there was a whole new generation of artists revisiting this idea of interior complexity, such as Jonathan Meese and John Bock.

It is important to point out that there is a strong link between how artists and architects respond to the Merzbau. In a nice fragment in the *Der Hang zum Gesamtkunstwerk* catalogue, Schwitters talks about architecture and Merz:

> I demand Merz architecture. This demand has two aspects: 1. Merz design in architecture. 2. Merzian application of architecture to create new form." More than any other category of art, architecture is intrinsically attuned to the Merz idea. As we know, Merz means the use of pre-existing old material to create a new work of art. Because of the unwieldiness of the materials with which houses are built, architecture had no other option than always to reuse the old and incorporate it into the new design.[1]

He is explicitly saying that he is not only making a claim for Merz architecture, but also that

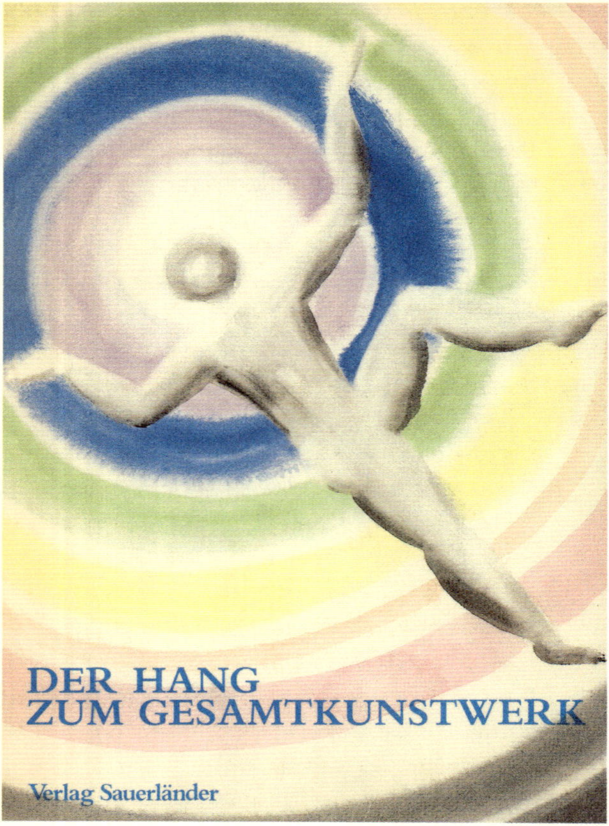

Book cover, *Der Hang zum Gesamtkunstwerk*, 1983, Verlag Sauerländer

architecture per se is mostly tuned into this idea of the "Merz thought."

A further important point is the question of the museum. The whole of the 1980s and 1990s have focused mainly on the facade of the museum, the exterior aspects, rather than on interior complexity. Nowadays there is a shift of paradigm, and interior complexity is becoming more important again, and more urgent in terms of museum architecture. We find a very striking example in the Herzog & De Meuron extension of the Walker Art Center that just opened in Minneapolis, with its focus on the program's interior community.

The Merzbau has always been in my mind as a kind of toolbox when working on time-based exhibitions, which in a way grew organically. Schwitters kept starting the Merzbau again and again, even after his emigration to Norway in 1937, and then after escaping to England. In each of those three contexts it was a sort of time-based growth. This principle has been very important for me. It was important to both Hou Hanru and myself when we made *Cities on the Move* (1990), and then also for Rirkrit Tiravanija, Molly Nesbit, and myself for *Utopia Station* (2003). We developed the idea that an exhibition might not just be something that happens for a month or two months and is then over, but is in fact a complex dynamic system with many feedback loops. It was also Schwitters who triggered the idea that the exhibition could just be a construction site, when he said, "it is unfinished and out of principle," and, "it grows according to the principles of the big city."[2] This whole analogy of the exhibition and the city played a role in the realization of *Cities on the Move* and *Utopia Station*.

The idea of the Merzbau and the city also became important for a project in Tirana. When Anri Sala and I were invited to curate a part of the Tirana Biennale, we spoke with the mayor Edi Rama—an artist who had become the mayor—who had actually decided to paint apartment-block walls in color geometries. He described this idea of large transformations of the city—creating a change—simply through the introduction of color. We then decided to invite artists to add to this Edi Rama list of buildings. Schwitters once said:

> Judicious excision of the most offensive parts, the inclusion of ugly and beautiful buildings within an overriding rhythm, and sensitive distribution of the main accents, would together enable the metropolis to be transformed into a colossal

> work of Merz art." Even by painting the whole of Berlin following the plan of a Merz architect, who would magnanimously paint out whole districts and use light and color to emphasize a few centers, which of course would not coincide with the traffic centers, the will to turn even a major city into a Merz work of art could be documented.[3]

One of the main focus of the Symposium Merzbau is how to bridge the art world and the world of architecture, and how we can create dialogues between art and architecture. I have the feeling that the Merzbau can be an excellent trigger for this. I hope that this offers a platform for dialogue. The idea is that all of this might very well lead to a bigger international exhibition. Not necessarily an exhibition about the Merzbau, but one in which the Merzbau is, once again, a trigger. In this sense the discussion has only just begun.

Notes

1. *Kurt Schwitters, Das literarische Werke*, ed. Friedhelm Lach, DuMont Schauberg, Cologne 1973–1981, vol. 5, p. 95f.
2. Ibid., p. 343.
3. Ibid., p. 95f.

The Merzbau as a Spatial Device

Stefano Boeri

By using three definitions of the notion of Merzbau, I will sum up some reasons why I am convinced that this notion is strategically crucial in the field of contemporary art and architecture.

1. WORLD BUILDING

The first definition is in the field of design: nowadays we can observe buildings which are meant to be capable of attracting, governing, and exposing an amazing complexity and multiplicity of environments, landscapes, and further aspects of the external world. The capacity of governing, attracting, and proposing a world within a single, unique object is becoming very important in the development of contemporary architecture. Furthermore, it is prominent in the recent practice of exhibition spaces produced by architects all over the world.

2. UNCERTAINTY

The second aspect is that of all of these complex experiences with "world buildings" have, at the same time, a certain degree of uncertainty, of incomplete determination, an incomplete definition of the building itself. Moreover, in today's architecture we can make out the awareness that the world, the notion of complexity, is strongly related to the notion of uncertainty. We have to establish a state of things to be capable of accepting the uncertainty of the future. We should accept variation and addition, that a multitude of subjects can continuously be introduced in our structure, in our scheme.

3. BREAKING THE SCALES

The third possible declination is that the notion of Merzbau is not only connected with a domestic space, although we can more often observe this Merzbau dynamic in spaces having a precise and small physical configuration. However, at the same time, this notion is nowadays breaking down the difference between design scale, interior architectural scale, architectural scale, and public space scale. From this point of view we should conceive of the Merzbau as a sort of spacial device, which is in fact working in our contemporary environment, trying to complexify these realities, to open all of these realities to the future, to introduce the notion of uncertainty.

All this is happening without a clear subdivisional scale. This has nothing to do with the small, large, or extra large dimension of a building. It rather has to do with the notion of device, which is today absolutely crucial in the architectural discussion. I mean device in the structural sense, as a tool, a specific tool being capable of transforming a building into something which is in turn capable of adapting itself to the change of things, of playing a dynamic role in our environment. If we want to use the idea of Merzbau within architectural practice and within artistic practice and discussion, we have to conceive of this notion as a sort of possible device.

From this point of view, when working in this sort of Merzbau sphere, it is important to focus on the capacity of this Merzbau environment to produce new ideas, new design concepts, new proposals. This capacity to generate is strongly connected with the dimension of design, the dimension of the designing processes, and projecting new ideas on the environment. From this perspective, Merzbau can really work as an internal device, it can be a creative device, it can produce change, it can produce transformation, it can produce steps in the development of our thoughts.

At this point we can start collecting different declinations of the notion of Merzbau as a device of change, as a device of designing new concepts and new processes.

Chapter One: Processed

The Merzbau and Expressionist Architecture

Dietmar Elger

In the context of Kurt Schwitters' achievement as a whole, the Merzbau has a unique and very prominent position. Not one of the artist's other enterprises, once under way, was pushed ahead with such total dedication. However, when we set out to describe, analyze, and evaluate the Merzbau, we still have to bear in mind that our subject remains no more than a fragment, and only ever existed in interim forms and in an imperfect state. Kurt Schwitters started constructing the Merzbau four times: after the first project was launched in Hanover, he made two separate attempts at it in Norway during the 1930s, and then tried for the fourth and last time in 1947 in England, in the Lake District. The Hanover building was destroyed in 1943 in an Allied bombing raid. Of the two structures erected in Norway, one fell victim to fire, the other to adverse weather. Only the fourth and last building remain, still incomplete, accommodated in a former barn and accordingly named the "Merzbarn."

This state of *incompleteness* is of the essence of all four of the buildings. The artist never envisaged a conclusion to the project in the sense of a finished building. The Merzbau remained unfinished "as a matter of principle," Schwitters insisted. If the dire political circumstances that attended his life had not driven him out of Hanover and subsequently out of his chosen country of adoption, Norway, Schwitters would have spent his entire remaining life continuing to work on his original Merzbau in Hanover—which by the early 1930s was just beginning to grow beyond the confines of the studio and spill over into other parts of his parental home at Waldhausenstrasse 5a.

When the Berlin Dadaists denied Kurt Schwitters from Hanover admission to membership of their elitist Club Dada, he promptly responded by founding his own one-man art movement under the name of Merz. He took the name from an assemblage that he had just produced, the so-called "Merzbild" [Merz picture]. This was the first appearance of the term "Merz" as a

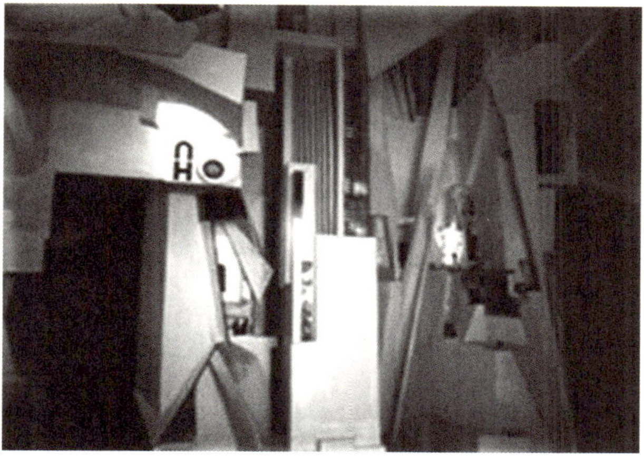

KURT SCHWITTERS *Merzbau*, Hanover, photographed in 1933 by Wilhelm Redemann

linguistic fragment. He had simply lifted it from a company name, "Privat- und Commerzbank."

From this point on, Schwitters rallied all his multifarious artistic activities under this nom de guerre. He would refer to his collages and assemblages as Merz drawings and Merz pictures. He produced numerous Merz sculptures and voluminous Merz poetry. He worked out the theory of Merz architecture—utopian in character—and reconstructed his studio as a fantasy Merz building [Merzbau].

The first monograph devoted to the Merz artist was published in 1966 by Werner Schmalenbach, founding director of the North Rhine-Westphalia State Art Collection in Düsseldorf. In it, Schmalenbach describes the Merzbau as an "Expressionist-Dadaist-Constructivist fantasy in the spirit of Dr. Caligari." This lapidary formulation does indeed identify the various formal inputs of which the Merzbau is constructed, although over the years each had come to partly mask the contribution of the others. The Merzbau had a bit of everything—not forgetting Expressionist cinema, of which the most noted example, *The Cabinet of Dr. Caligari*, 1920, is rightly adduced here by Schmalenbach.

Kurt Schwitters was never going to be one of the great innovators, formally or graphically. His special gift lay in acquiring material—which might very well consist in a particular art style—and then re-working it and integrating it into his Merz art. Immediately after the war ended, Schwitters had adopted this "Merz principle" as his working method: "The whole place was in ruins, and the thing was to take the rubble and build something new. That's all Merz is about."

Any random objects that came his way, and similarly any current aesthetic or stylistic fashion, such as Expressionism or Constructivism, might serve him as the stonemason's quarry from which he would hew material for his new Merz art. In a late letter, written in 1946 to Raoul Hausmann, one of his few Dadaist comrades-in-arms, Schwitters drew an astonishing comparison: "When it's that crook Picasso, you want to know what artist he's plagiarising today. But if it's about me, you ask what I've been re-working today." As far as the Merzbau was concerned, this applied particularly to the ideas Schwitters drew from Expressionist architecture. An American author, Rosemarie Haag Bletter, writing in 1977, went so far as to declare the Merzbau "the only truly Expressionist building ever executed."

Expressionist architecture was a characteristic phenomenon of those years in the immediate aftermath of the Great War when not only the architects, but many others, were seeking a fresh start for society as a whole. Their minds still possessed by the terrible slaughter and by the horrors of the European battlegrounds, and disappointed by society and politics, these architects designed their utopian buildings for remote and untouched places among high mountains. “Alpine Architecture” and the Gothic cathedral were their inspiration. After the wartime hatred among peoples, the hope was that the youth of Europe would come together in a spirit of amity and joint endeavor to build these new cathedrals and places of meditation and prayer.

Bruno Taut, born in Königsberg in 1880, became the leading theoretician and the active organizing force at the center of the little group of Expressionist architects. Having completed his academic training in his native city, Taut practiced initially in Berlin, then in Stuttgart. In 1909, back in Berlin, he launched an architectural practice of his own. During the next few years he oversaw the construction of several residential and industrial buildings as well as terraced housing for the Falkenberg garden city project. However, his most important contract was the glass building he designed in 1914 for the Werkbund exhibition in Cologne. On this project he collaborated with the Expressionist poet Paul Scheerbarth, who provided a frieze encircling the building with 14 terse aphorisms. One of these read: “Das Glas bringt uns die neue Zeit, Backsteinkultur tut uns nur leid” (which can be approximately paraphrased as “In glass we see our bright tomorrow; in bricks and mortar, former sorrow”). The message directly over the entrance read: “Das bunte Glas Zerstört den Haß” (“Glass banishes, Hatred vanishes”).

The crystalline architecture of the glass building erected in the last few pre-war months, and Scheerbarth’s somewhat naive Salvationism, mark this structure as an early herald of the utopian concepts dreamed up by post-1918 Expressionist architecture. During the war and for some years afterward, civil construction in Germany virtually ceased. Eventually, out of economic necessity, Bruno Taut had no option but to take employment as an editor on the journal *Stadtbaukunst Alter und Neuer Zeit* (City Architecture Old and New), taking charge of the *Frühlicht* (First Light) supplement. From January to July 1920 there were 14 editions of this supplement, all of them intended to provide architects, especially the rising generation, with a forum for theory and debate. Dismissed by the journal's editorial board, Taut carried on publishing *Frühlicht* as a journal in its own right. But between autumn 1921 and summer 1922 only a further four independent issues appeared.

It had been back in November 1919 that Taut invited a number of his architect friends to exchange ideas by letter. Addressing his circular to his "Dear Colleagues," he put the following proposal to them: "At the present time there is almost no building work to be had, and if we are once in a while given the chance to build, we only do it to stay alive. Or have you perhaps been so fortunate as to land a nice commission? By now I have almost no stomach for practice, and by and large I daresay it is the same with you. To be honest, it is really something of a blessing that there is no building work in progress anywhere at present. This is a time for slow maturing; we are gathering our strength, and when in due course everything starts to move again, we will know where we want to go, and we will be strong enough to safeguard our movement against all that is gimcrack and degenerate. Let us be 'architects of the imagination' and proud of it!"

Seeking to underline the intimate character of the correspondence, Taut suggested to his confreres

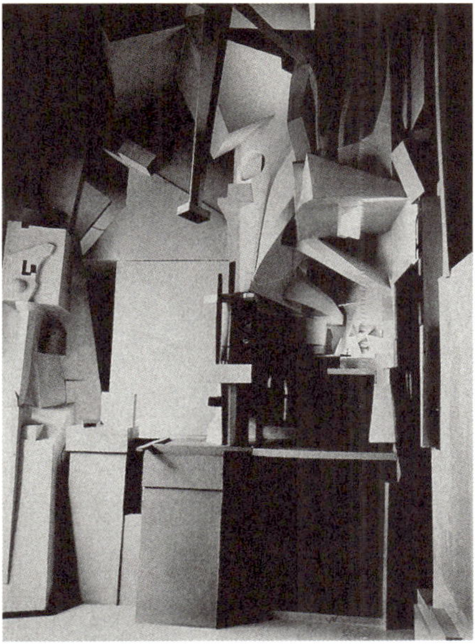

KURT SCHWITTERS *Merzbau*, Hanover, photographed in 1933 by Wilhelm Redemann

in the *Gläserne Kette* (Glass Chain) that they should all use pseudonyms. For himself he chose the name *Glas* (Glass), alluding back to the humanistic ideals that inspired his glass architecture of 1914. Apart from Taut, the Glass Chain numbered 12 architects, including the brothers Hans and Wassili Luckhardt, respectively styled "Angkor" and "Zacken" (Jagged Line). Hans Scharoun chose the sobriquet "Hannes," while Hermann Finsterlin hid behind the name "Prometh," and Walter Gropius rather soberly went for "Mass" (Moderation or Measure). Wenzel Hablik flatly refused to adopt a pseudonym, confining himself in the correspondence to signing with his initials, W.H.

In the second letter he wrote to his circle of friends, which is dated December 27, 1919, Bruno Taut again stressed the personal and confidential nature of their exchange of ideas; yet at the same time he also imparted the news that he would be publishing excerpts from their private letters in the *Frühlicht* journal supplement of which he was to become editor in the following month. He wrote: "Prometh is quite right—we must take great care to safeguard the seeds of the future. That means no announcements of 'action plans.' Only rare publications, and those exclusive. No references to 'Our group'! Let us not have our long-term objectives smothered in mere activity and reduced to the humdrum. A public profile only where it is needed to attract related spirits. These are the principles by which my *Frühlicht* is governed."

Subsequently, it was by way of the later, independent issues of *Frühlicht* that the architects were put in touch with the Merz artist of Hanover, Kurt Schwitters.

On December 20, 1921, Schwitters wrote a letter to an artist friend, Walter Dexel, with whom he had collaborated in organizing a Dadaist evening in Jena the previous July, thanking Dexel for bringing a press notice to his attention: "Many thanks for drawing my attention to a review I had not seen in *Frühlicht*—do please always keep me posted on such things." The issue referred to could only have been the first of the independently produced *Frühlicht* numbers, which appeared in autumn 1921.

Schwitters must have got hold of a copy of the journal and studied it with interest, and probably likewise the following issue of *Frühlicht*, dated winter 1921/1922, as the third independent number, published in spring 1922, featured an article written by Schwitters himself. It took the form of a manifesto and was entitled “Schloß und Kathedrale mit Hofbrunnen” (Castle and Cathedral with Courtyard Well). In this piece and in his reproduction of an architectural model, he puts forward his own theoretical thinking on architecture, alongside the utopias of the Expressionist architects.

Even externally, in its architectural structure, in the interlocking cubes, the soaring and plunging rib features, and the many jostling projections and recesses, the Merzbau exhibits clear formal affinities with the works of the Expressionist architects. At the same time, none of the latters' many utopian drawings and sketches, and none of the few buildings that were erected, can be seriously compared with the Merzbau in terms of overall design. However, similarities do exist in a host of multifarious details. While Expressionist architecture tended to polarize, toward an organic structural concept on the one hand, and a crystalline one on the other, Schwitters' Merzbau actually incorporates the stylistic and theoretical features of both trends. And where the Expressionist architects saw their ideal in the collective undertaking that was the cathedral, for Schwitters, by contrast, the Merzbau might indeed be a cathedral but was—in his words—a “cathedral of erotic misery,” and thus the shrine of his purely personal mythologizing.

Comparison of certain examples of unrealized Expressionist architectural projects dating from the 1918–1921 period—for instance Max Taut's *Blütenhaus* (House of Blossoms, 1921) or Hermann Finsterlin's *Haus der Andacht–Museum* (House of Meditation and Prayer–Museum, 1919) —shows what are at the very least startling resemblances to Schwitters' Merzbau, though only in the form it had assumed by the beginning of the 1930s.

The few examples of Expressionist architecture that were actually built include Walter Gropius' *Denkmal für die Märzgefallenen* (Memorial to the March Dead, 1920–1921) in Weimar, the rebuilding of the Berlin *Scala-Tanzpalast* (Scala Dance Palace) by Walter Würzbach and the sculptor Rudolf Belling, in 1920, and the advertisement structures at the Avus in Berlin, of 1922–1923. In the last of these, Belling collaborated with the architect Wassili Luckhardt, who in his role as a Glass Chain member hid behind the pseudonym of "Zacken." Kurt Schwitters can hardly have failed to be aware of these projects. One photograph from the Merzbau even shows a label with "Theater Scala" inscribed on it.

In the third independent number of Bruno Taut's journal *Frühlicht*, "Eine Folge für die Verwirklichung des neuen Baugedankens," which came out in spring 1922, Kurt Schwitters published a photograph of the architectural model called "Schloß und Kathedrale mit Hofbrunnen" and juxtaposed his own theory of what he called Merz architecture with the utopias of the Expressionist architects. Schwitters began his piece with a little anecdote about how his wife had collected the model from the photographer's and found herself having to explain during the tram journey home what she was carrying. According to Schwitters, she explained that it was a castle, a church, and a well that her young son had nailed together—a white lie that earned her the collective approbation of her fellow passengers, and praise from the conductor, who considered that the lad had a fine healthy imagination.

Old urban buildings, he maintained, should no longer be pulled down wholesale, destroyed, and replaced by new buildings; rather, old and new architecture should be integrated into a new superordinate whole.

In a very similar vein, Paul Wolf—Hanover's chief planning and buildings officer at the time—was writing in his *Das hohe Ufer* (*High Bank by Water*) about introducing the concept of rhythm into city planning: "The function of urban planning taken as a whole is to integrate all the elements of architectural and physical form and meld them into the overall rhythm of street and square, park and cemetery, forming the total artwork that is the city." Bruno Taut likewise, with his two pro-jects, *The City Crown* and *Alpine Architecture*, both 1919, was aiming to create nothing less than the perfectly pre-planned urban design.

Kurt Schwitters had already built his own first architectural model called *Haus Merz*, in 1920. This *Haus Merz*, too, was a cathedral, chock-full of cogwheels, and featuring a button as a clock face on the tower. At the time, Schwitters did not comment personally on this project, preferring to use a friend, the Hanover journalist Christof Spengemann, as his mouthpiece. In an article entitled "Merz—the Official Art," Spengemann articulates exactly what was in Schwitters' mind: "In his piece called *Haus Merz*, Kurt Schwitters has opened up a new field in which to deploy his art: that of architecture. Of the architecture that is not mere building for a purpose. I see, in *Haus Merz*, the cathedral. The cathedral. Not church architecture. No, but rather the building as expression of the truly spiritual contemplation of the one thing that puts us in touch with Infinity: absolute Art."

For the Expressionist architects too, the highest ideal was represented by the cathedral, a structure without utilitarian purpose, reserved solely for spiritual contemplation. Back in 1914, speaking of his glass building in Cologne, Bruno Taut had claimed: "This building does not need to have any purely practical function. Architecture too can cast off the utilitarian shackles." In the catalogue that accompanied the Werkbund exhibition, he added: "The glass building has no other function than to be beautiful." However, in his *Alpine Architecture* Taut formulated still more precisely what it was that he expected architecture to provide: "The cathedral's function? None at all—if the contemplation of beauty does not suffice."

Kurt Schwitters knew as well as anyone that his Merz architecture was purely utopian. The model called *Castle and Cathedral with Courtyard Well* was not a mock-up for the real thing, but was intended rather as stimulus material for the other architects: a model for thinkers rather than builders. "For refreshing the architectural imagination," as Schwitters explained in his accompanying essay.

The Glass Chain members too were clear about the utopian nature of projects like Taut's *Alpine Architecture* and Wenzel Hablik's *Air Colony*. For Bruno Taut, the visionary designs produced by the Glass Chain represented an experimental laboratory for trying out new architectural forms. And he called for the highest possible standards of aesthetic merit: "We must always know the unattainable and desire it, if we are to reach what is attainable."

At the beginning of the 1930s, Kurt Schwitters found himself facing the same situation that he had faced at the end of the 1914–1918 war. Once again he and his art had to respond to acute pressure from outside. Whereas in 1919 the imperative for him had been to construct a new artistic order out of the debris of the war, now he was struggling to escape from the harassments and the hostility to which he was increasingly subjected with the rise of National Socialism in Germany. This was the reason for his increasingly lengthy summer stays in Norway. During his remaining time in Hanover, too, he shut himself away more and more in his Merzbau. Over this period, which ended with his permanent emigration from Germany in January 1937, he fashioned it into a sealed-off, other-worldly cathedral, a piece of Alpine Architecture in the urban heart of Hanover.

For Schwitters, the Merzbau became a private place of refuge from the political radicalization of Germany. It was at once a tower and a cave. Both of these are architectural forms to which the Expressionist architects likewise turned when seeking spaces suitable for living in voluntary isolation.

Thus, while Schwitters the artist could not influence the course of great political and social changes, and had no desire to do so, he was, in the meantime, building himself his own quite separate world in the shape of the Merzbau. Here the world became amenable to his rule and could be ordered and manipulated to his heart's content in accordance with rules that he had drawn up himself. And this is precisely the playful approach to handling materials that Kurt Schwitters always claimed to be central to his art. "Taking weighty problems, and playing with them—that's what art is," he told his friend Raoul Hausmann in 1946. And in a letter written in the same year to his long-standing Hanover companion Christof Spengemann, it is there again, defiantly: "We play here until death comes to collect us."

Thorny Issues of Two-Dimensional Photographs and 3-Dimensional Reconstructions

Peter Bissegger in conversation with Dietmar Elger

DIETMAR ELGER In 1980, Harald Szeemann hit on the idea of getting the Merzbau reconstructed as a feature of the exhibition *Der Hang zum Gesamtkunstwerk* (*Tendencies Toward the Total Work of Art*). That was an extremely difficult undertaking—it was only thanks to Ernst Schwitters, the artist's son, that it was possible at all. With some help from Werner Schmalenbach it was agreed that it would be called a reconstruction, an attempt at reconstruction. At that point Harald Szeemann first spoke to Peter Bissegger, who was to realize the project. And for many years now the reconstruction has been on display in the Sprengel Museum in Hanover.

PETER BISSEGGER The reason this Merzbau happened was actually that I'm not good at saying no. Soon after Harald Szeemann first spoke to me about it, he contacted me again to say that Ernst Schwitters was coming to see me. I still hadn't a clue what the Merzbau was all about. So on Szeemann's advice I rushed off post-haste to the Kunsthaus library in Zurich. And there, for the

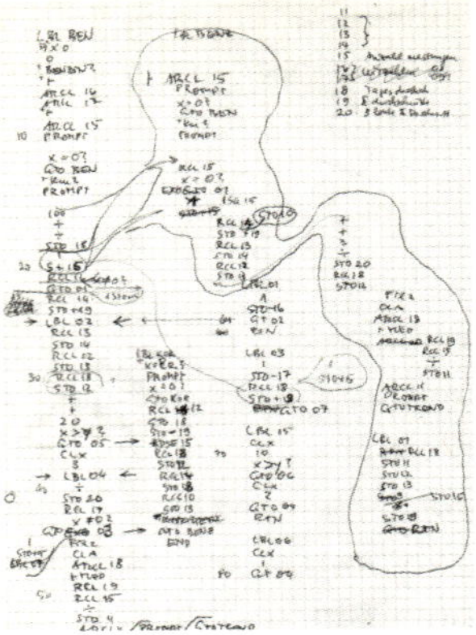

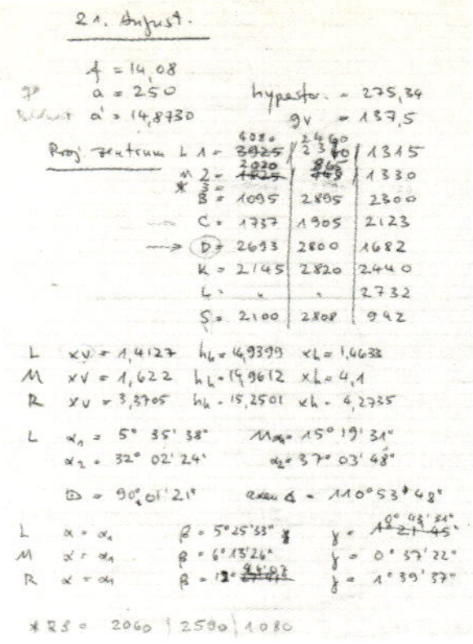

PETER BISSEGGER *HP 41*, 1982, calculation program for iterary sequence (the infinite approximation)

PETER BISSEGGER *21 August*, 1982, final result of the calculations for three dimensional reconstruction

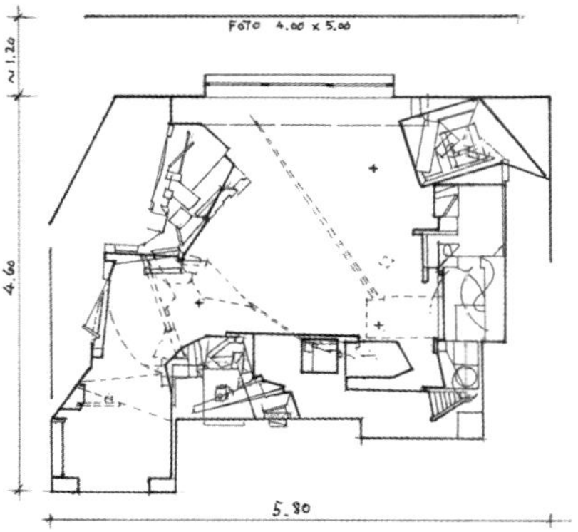

PETER BISSEGGER *Grundriss Merzbau*, 2005, floor plan of the Merzbau in the actual room

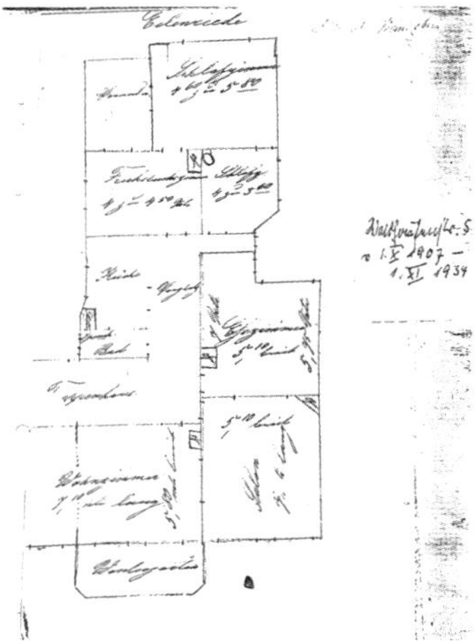

PETER BISSEGGER *Grundriss Grossvater*, 1907, floor plan of the Schwitters Family flat at Waldenhausstr. 5A in Hanover, drawing by the father of Kurt Schwitters

first time, I got a clear idea of the simply enormous dimensions of this project. Consequently, when I talked to Ernst Schwitters, I had to try and bluff my way through. I talked about reasoning things out by analogy and so on, and it must have seemed persuasive to Ernst Schwitters, so I then had no option but to do it.

Essentially, all we had to go on right at the beginning, our only evidence, was the three photographs dating from 1933. Then there was another photograph from the journal *Abstraction*, and a number of snapshots taken by Ernst and several other people. These showed various aspects of the Merzbau, which were not shown in the three photographs we had. And that was it. Some plans of the apartment came to light. I was familiar with the ground plan, but I didn't know the height. And I knew what kind of camera had been used to take the photographs, but we still had to find out what the focal length had been.

DIETMAR ELGER When you have so little to go on, there is bound to be an issue over how far off you'll be. All you've got is two-dimensional photographs, and you're supposed to construct a three-dimensional model from what they tell you. You've got black-and-white photos, and you're supposed to make a full-color model. And on top of that you had to find out what the scale was.

How could you possibly get the answers to all that?

PETER BISSEGGER Well, to start with, a whole lot of features appear on two of the photographs. But there is only a single point that appears on all three, and this gave us the continuous sequence from far left to far right. That enabled me to calculate the three-dimensional model. In terms of the colors, Ernst Schwitters gave me the help I needed. He'd been ten years old when his father started building the Merzbau, and 17 at the end, and so naturally he knew the Merzbau inside out. He had even helped a bit in the construction work. When we were building the model he followed me round inside it continuously for four days, making me fine-tune each shade until he felt it was what the original had been. So the colors we have are Ernst Schwitters' work. It was obvious he knows the building intimately, and I just trusted him. Of course, objective proof is another matter, I don't have that. Ernst Schwitters actually also said that to start with there had been more colors. Schwitters senior apparently changed everything to white when they were finished, except for the colors we see now on the photographs of the rebuild. And then after those photographs had been taken, he painted the whole thing over again, in white, and using matte oil paint—even the floor. Visitors were made to wear slippers he kept ready just outside the door, partly so that they didn't have to keep repainting the floor, but in part also to ensure that when they went in they did so with all due respect.

DIETMAR ELGER How did you prove you had it right when you finished? Were you able, so-to-speak, to re-take these three photos using your model?

PETER BISSEGGER The original camera had a focal length of 14.1 cm. It was a Protar, which meant it was an extreme wide-angle camera. At the Institute of Photography at the ETH (Eidgenössische Technische Hochschule, the Technical University of Zurich) I found a reference to a Protar by Zeiss that had a 14.1 cm lens. Using this appropriate instrument, I constructed specific box shapes. You can do this because these cameras are dropped plate cameras. They lend themselves very well to optical manipulation. If you repeat the original manipulations, and use this lens to take a picture from the identical spot, then it will match up exactly. I took two photographs.

I do know that five or six things are wrong. I had a set of prints made by a professional photographer, developed to a whole range of shades from very light to very dark, and these

Hausbogen

Waldhausenstr. 5A

Eigentümer :

Erdgeschoss : v. Wartensleben, Regierungsrat.

Die Wohnung ist ausgenützt.

I. Stock : Geisse, Regierungsbaurat.

Von einer Zwangseinmietung ist abzusehen.

Hausbogen, Waldhausenstr. 5A, date unknown

32

Serie V. Anastigmat 1 : 18.

Weitwinkelobjectiv für Architekturen, Innenräume und photogrammetrische Aufnahmen, sowie Objectiv für Reproductionen.

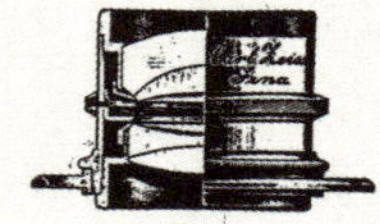

Fig. 10.
Anastigmat 1 : 18 f = 632 mm
Serie V No. 9.
(In ⅔ natürlicher Grösse.)

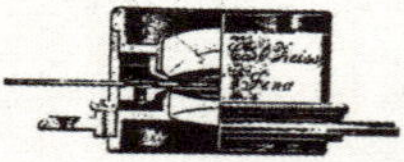

Fig. 11.
Anastigmat 1 : 18 f = 141 mm
Serie V No. 3.
(In natürlicher Grösse.)

Die kleinen Nummern des Anastigmaten 1 : 18 (bis zur Brennweite 390 mm) besitzen einen Bildwinkel von über 110°, sie sind demnach im eigentlichen Sinne Weitwinkelsysteme. Ihre Oeffnung 1 : 18 genügt für die meisten Arten von Momentaufnahmen im Freien bei Sonnenlicht. Die Zeichnung ist gut orthoskopisch, sodass das Objectiv auch für photogrammetrische Zwecke in erster Linie in Betracht zu ziehen ist.

Die grösseren Brennweiten (von 460 mm ab) haben ein Gesichtsfeld von etwa 90°, sie sind im Besonderen für Reproductionen bestimmt. Das Bildfeld ist daher für eine Ausdehnung von ca. 60° besonders gut anastigmatisch geebnet.

Serie und No.	Aequivalent-Brennweite mm	Linsendurchmesser mm	Empfehlenswert bei Blende 1 : 18 für das Plattenformat cm	Empfehlenswert bei Blende 1 : 36 für das Plattenformat cm	Durchmesser des scharfen Feldes bei kl. Blenden cm	Objectiv in Messingfassung mit Iris: Preis M.	Objectiv in Messingfassung mit Iris: Telegrammwort	Serie und No.
V, 0	40	3.5	4.5 × 6	6 × 8	10.5	64	Laban	V, 0
V, 00	62	5	6 × 8	8 × 10	14.5	64	Labe	V, 00
V, 1	86	7.5	9 × 12	12 × 15	22	64	Labrador	V, 1
V, 2	112	9.5	12 × 15	13 × 18	28	64	Lagune	V, 2
V, 3	141	12	13 × 18	16 × 21	36	80	Lama	V, 3
V, 4	182	14.5	16 × 21	20 × 26	40	100	Lapsus	V, 4
V, 5	212	17.5	20 × 26	24 × 30	54	125	Lateran	V, 5
V, 6	265	20.5	24 × 30	26 × 35	68	155	Lava	V, 6
V, 7	315	23.5	26 × 35	30 × 40	80	185	Lawine	V, 7
V, 7a	390	26	30 × 40	40 × 50	85	245	Leda	V, 7a
V, 8	460	26	30 × 40	40 × 50	84	245	Legende	V, 8
V, 9	632	35	40 × 50	60 × 70	116	360	Legion	V, 9
V, 10	947	54	50 × 60	80 × 90	173	710	Leo	V, 10

Grössere Nummern werden nur auf besondere Bestellung angefertigt.

Description of Protar objective by Zeiss, appox. 1890, Nachlass Photographisches Institut, ETH Bibliothek, Zurich

showed up two things that I could not see on my own prints. For instance, there is a small doll or puppet in front of one of the boxes, and you can only see it on the least developed of the photographs. But when I found that it was too late. And there is a bit of plaster missing on the window. If Schwitters made plaster and then forgot about it, he would just ram it in anywhere. That happened in two places in the original, and one of them was missed out in the first reconstruction. I do have it now in the copy of the reconstruction.

Still, when the attempt at reconstruction of the Merzbau was finished, Ernst Schwitters said: ‘That’s a dream come true!’ He had been feeling it was crazy the building did not exist any more, and now he was just overjoyed.

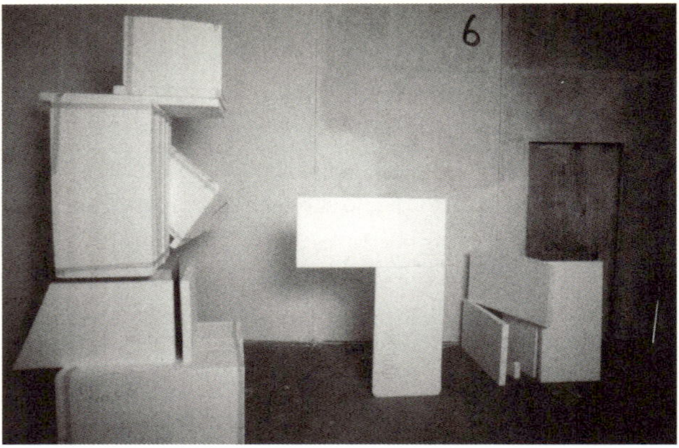

PETER BISSEGGER *Anfang*, 1982, first attempts to make a model of the Merzbau

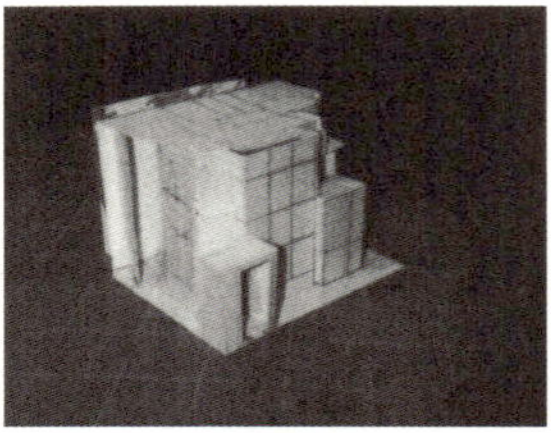

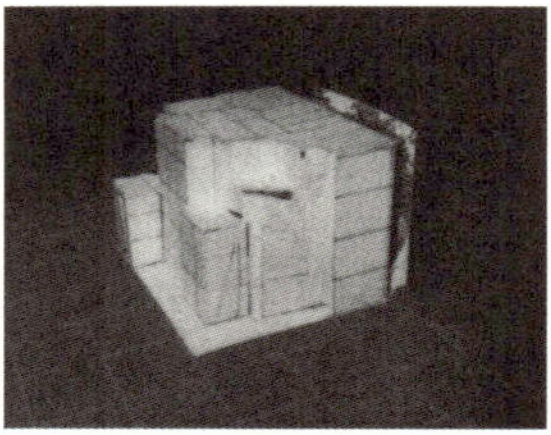

PETER BISSEGGER *Modell*, 1988, model of the reconstruction of the Merzbau

The Merzbau as Gesamtkunstwerk

Gwendolen Webster

Kurt Schwitters' Hanover Merzbau, which he regarded as his most significant work, was destroyed in 1943. In exile in far-off London, he made desperate plans to rescue and restore its desolate remains, but finally had to admit that his plans were futile. "My studio and my life's work no logner exist," he wrote in 1945. "And I go on living ... isn't it sad. What did I actually live for? I don't know." It was a tragedy for Schwitters, but despite his predictions, the Merzbau has continued to survive and flourish in endless books, articles, and projects, while providing a fine opportunity for art historians to theorize endlessly without the presence of the original to prove them wrong. Here it is my turn to theorize, and, as this book is dedicated to the memory of Harald Szeemann, I shall base my essay on his 1994 text "Zum Gesamtkunstwerk von Kurt Schwitters" (Kurt Schwitters' Total Work of Art), part of which was published in the catalogue of Szeemann's best-known exhibition, *Der Hang zum Gesamtkunstwerk* (Tendencies Toward the Total Work of Art, 1983).

Szeemann regards the Gesamtkunstwerk as in effect unrealizable—all to the good, he maintains, for the concept carries a propensity for the unconditional and the absolute that finds its most ominous expression in a rigid system or a political dystopia. Having presented us with the negative, sinister aspects of the Gesamtkunstwerk when accompanied by the desire to exert complete control, Szeemann chooses to focus on the striving for the Gesamtkunstwerk rather than its attainment. He visualizes the Hang zum Gesamtkunstwerk as a "poetic zone of thought constructions," a space in which an individual may develop total creative freedom, and paints a whimsical picture of a realm in which such disparate figures as Goethe, Runge, Scriabin, Rudolf Steiner, Kandinsky, Mondrian, Malevich, Taut, and Josef Beuys live in harmony, with nothing in common apart from an obsessive ambition to create a total work of art.

Szeemann naturally includes Schwitters in this company and points to the Hanover Merzbau as an example of the Hang zum Gesamtkunstwerk. This is not mere theorizing; the idea was at least suggested by Schwitters himself and by a number of his contemporaries, in particular Carola Giedion-Welcker, the only professional art historian to visit the Merzbau before writing about it.

In 1947 she stated that "[Schwitters'] aim from the first was a Gesamtkunstwerk in which all the arts were to be united in this Merz construction ... to build a monumental, condensed, artistic synthesis of our time. The foundations of a realization of this idea were put into practice by Schwitters in the interior extensions of his studio, where he built an endless Merz column into which he injected a never-ending stream of new witticisms, fanciful ideas, fantastic forms and objects."

Projects that aimed at a synthesis of the arts were of course commonplace in Schwitters' time, though the concept was by no means new. Perhaps the most influential statement on the comprehensive integration of the arts was formulated by Richard Wagner in his 1849 essay *The Artwork of the Future*. This is the utopian, romantic view of the Gesamtkunstwerk, which assumes that beneath the various forms of creative activity there lies a common identity representative of some higher truth, which, when revealed, will point to a new social order. Wagner's desire to create the Gesamtkunstwerk involved an idiosyncratic philosophy which was praised by some and condemned by others; George Bernard Shaw saw *The Ring Cycle* as a revolutionary call to the masses, Nietzsche and

Adorno found the concept behind Wagner's music indigestible and dogmatic, and the arguments about the ideological aspects of Wagner's operas persist to this day. Perhaps, then, it is not so easy to distinguish between the negative Gesamtkunstwerk and the positive Hang zum Gesamtkunstwerk, as Szeemann would have us believe.

In 1865, August Pecht painted a portrait of Wagner, which, with its chiaroscuro effects and its upwardly curving gesture, perfectly embodied the composer's endeavor, and I would like to stay with the gesture as one of the most effective ways of imparting structure and meaning to the abstract concept of the Hang zum Gesamtkunstwerk; the gesture in the widest sense may be regarded as that which articulates the spatial coordinates of the Gesamtkunstwerk. Fifty years before Wagner's composition, Philip Otto Runge's painting *The Lesson of the Nightingale*, based on a poem and, as Runge tells us, composed according to fugal principles, expressed his personal idea of the Gesamtkunstwerk—art combined with literature and music—in terms of an organic gesture. As Wagner built the opera house at Bayreuth to contain his Gesamtkunstwerk, so Runge also envisaged a building, a kind of sanctuary, for his synthesis of the arts, but died too young to complete more than a few sketches.

When describing the Merzbau in a brief essay of 1933, Schwitters made reference to what he termed "the most important of my forms"—the half spiral, which can be seen in many of the stalactite-like constructions of the Hanover Merzbau. The arc may be categorized as one of the dynamic gestures espoused by the Modernist artists of the early 20th century as an expression of their utopian aspirations, and was accordingly distrusted by Fascism, which favored instead the stringency implicit in its authoritarian worldview. Mussolini was, however, not above appropriating the dynamic gesture for his own purposes. In the 1932 exhibition celebrating the tenth anniversary of the March on Rome, for instance, the visitor progressed through a series of 15 asymmetrical, disorientating rooms until reaching the final four rooms, linked by a corridor and reminiscent of a cathedral nave; here the constructions began to take recognizable form, and stabilized until one reached the shadowy Hall of Martyrs, a vision of absolute order and symmetry. Here, then, Fascism effectively deployed the dynamic gesture to illustrate the intermediate stage between revolution and regime. In Hitler's Third Reich, which tried to obliterate the concept of revolution (implying rivalry), such use of instability was out of the question. National Socialist ideology deployed the symmetrical and the frozen, the monumental, rigidly determined gesture, in architecture as in art. In the 1920s, it was the avant-garde's distortions of the human figure that critics seized upon as indicative of mental aberration. In the following decade, warped space and the dynamic gesture were demoted to the realm of the Untermensch, the subhuman creature. In Ludwig Clauss' *Rasse und Seele* of 1933—just one of the early 20th century's flood of books on supposed racial hierarchies—the human figure, whether in art or reality, is treated like a waxwork. Body language is frozen for analysis in photos, whereby physical distortions are interpreted as moral indicators; the deviation from the upright is to be understood in both a literal and a metaphorical sense. Clauss juxtaposes the submissive, apologetic gesture of a Jew and the twists and turns of non-German politicians addressing their voters, with the stiff-backed stance of the Nordic male, who is thus perceived to belong to a powerful, superior race. Likewise, the disfigurations of the human body prevalent in modernist art gave rise to constant right-wing censure. Schwitters' Merz pictures were abstract, but the implication of the artist as rag-picker was sufficient to damn him in the view of his early critics, and in the *Entartete Kunst* exhibition of 1937, his original Merz picture was hung askew, a gesture designed to underscore the artist's deformed worldview.

The gaze directed downward was, as we know from his friends, Schwitters' most characteristic personal gesture—his continual search for those fragments of rubbish that he first used in his Merz picture of 1919. I'd like to consider how Schwitters developed his idea of the total work of art from this first assemblage, because in his first Merz manifesto of 1919, he outlined no more than a method of painting, of creating a framed work that can be signed. He quickly extended his technique of collage, however, to include prose, poetry, sculpture, drama, architecture, and of course his own Merz magazine; the result was a form of intermediary art where objects situated in one practice are open to interpretation in terms of another. Schwitters' work often becomes almost impossible to categorize—his *Ursonate* is open to analysis as poetry or music, other poems take the form of pictures or prose, images are also texts, letters and numbers become abstract structures, and Schwitters' mythical heroine Anna Blume crops up everywhere. Additionally, any Merz work may also be regarded as a fragment and thus as material for a further Merz work; we find, for instance, Schwitters collaging his own typographical designs for the municipal authorities of Hanover. As Szeemann explains, Schwitters' concept of the Gesamtkunstwerk extends far beyond that of his contemporaries such as Kandinsky: Merz does not imply the temporal play of all the arts, but rather creates an indeterminate space in which traditional art forms are redefined or even rendered irrelevant. Having learned from Dada a method of breaking down the boundaries between art and non-art, Schwitters finally identifies himself with his art and begins to call himself Merz. As Szeemann notes, in his memoirs, Hans Richter concluded it was not Merz, but Schwitters himself, who constituted the total work of art.

The basis for the Merz Gesamtkunstwerk, as Schwitters tells us, is the Merzgesamtweltbild, the Merz total world picture: "Merz means establishing relationships, best of all between all the things in the world." If such a universal claim, coupled with the identification of art and artist, sounds like a megalomaniac's proposition, Szeemann reminds us that the Merzbau, with its content of refuse and its location in a obscure back room, should be compared with what he describes as a classic example of the Hang zum Gesamtkunstwerk; Gabriele D'Annunzio's pompous, hugely ostentatious *Vittoriale degli Italiani* citadel (1921–1938) on Lake Garda. In this theater of memory, constructed in just the period that Schwitters was working on the Merzbau, we find the grand gesture; the monument D'Annunzio built to himself as hero; "Everything here," he wrote, "is characterized by my style ... that is, by my love for Italy, my cult of memory, my strivings for heroism, my vision of a Fatherland of the future ... Everything here is an aspect of my soul, proof of my burning dedication." Needless to say, Schwitters' rare expressions of nationalist sentiment invariably took a quite different, subversive form; "I assure you that all the pieces of material that I use are purely German, collected on German rubbish heaps."

Schwitters' earliest theoretical text on the Gesamtkunstwerk (which exists in several versions) is the *Merzbühne*, the Merz stage, which Szeemann quotes from extensively in his essay. Schwitters' forceful introduction reads like a manifesto: "I demand the Merz stage. I demand the complete combination of all artistic forces in the attainment of the total work of art. I demand the principle of equality of all materials." It is noticeable, however, that the essay turns into a series of instructions or a handbook on how to construct his fantasy theater—in other words, he passes the gestures on to the reader. We are told to concoct the Merz stage as a vast, uncontrollable assemblage, by hurling dynamic lines and structures onto imploding and exploding surfaces, following them with a deluge of disfigured, hacked, strangled, and beheaded objects, including people, until the spectacle reaches a menacing, orgasmic climax with the squirting of foam.

"Take giant surfaces, conceived as infinite, cloak them in color, twist and push them around menacingly, disfigure their smooth shamefulness ... Bend the lines, crank and crook angles strangling whirls around a point ... Nets contain narrow the pain of Antonius ... Then take wheels and axles, hurl them up and make them sing ... Ratchet wheels sense ratchets, find a sewing machine that yawns. Screwing upward or hunkered down, the sewing machine beheads itself, feet up. Take a dentist's drill, a meat grinder, a trolley scraper, buses and automobiles, bicycles, tandems and their tires and deform them. Take lights and deform them in the most brutal manner. Explode steam boilers to make railroad smog ... Also take, and why not, man-traps, automatic pistols, infernal machines, the tin fish, and the funnel ... even people can be used. People can be tied to backdrops ... Now begin to wed these various materials to one another ... Feed the sphere to the surface and let a cracked corner be utterly destroyed by a 22-thousand candle-power arc light ... Foam is squirted .... Behind the stage set organs sing and say futt, futt ... The sewing machine screeches ahead ... Drums and flutes flash death ... A jet of ice-cold water in a pot runs down the back of the man perched on the backdrop ... a violin melody shimmers pure and tender as young girls ... Deep dark red the middle boils embers. Light darkens stage, even the sewing machine is dark."

This ultra-Futurist theater is, however, offset by the ironies of a text that constantly subverts its own aims by the use of paradox, self-parody, alienation effects, and cliché. Art critics take part as pudding molds, children are admitted half-price, and the reader, cast as a potential rapist, is confronted by a caricature and a reversal of the rapist's role, a cosmic sewing machine that finally cobbles the frenzied stage props together and is the last object to disappear as the Merz stage relapses into darkness. The Merz stage, however, as Schwitters admitted himself, was a fantasy. How does his version of the Gesamtkunstwerk develop from imagined space to real space, from literature to the concrete constructions of the Merzbau?

Let us look at space as Schwitters the student saw it in his 1910 painting of a domestic interior

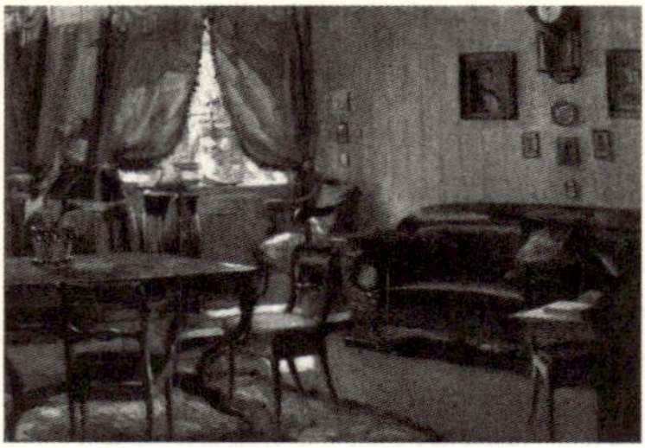

KURT SCHWITTERS *Untitled (Interior)*, about 1910, oil on canvas, 62.5 x 86.5 cm, private collection (which we may assume was in his parents' apartment or that of close relations). Here the outside world is almost shut out, and the room prefers to reflect itself in the mirror, the furniture—you can almost smell the furniture polish—and even the leaves of the inhospitably spiky potted plant, and a book, read by someone who prefers to shun the light from the window. The living are notable by their absence; only the dead are present, in the fuzzy ancestors' portraits on the wall. These pictures are, however, somewhat misleading. Schwitters' parents were working-class nouveau riche, and their profession was centered around the shop window, the open gaze, the world of commodities; the Schwitters' family was not born into this polished, immaculate world of the front parlor; in a sense, then, we are looking at a gesture of self-deception.

A few years later, after his invention of Merz, we see Schwitters portrayed as a solemn figure in an oppressive domestic setting, with his wife Helma cast in the role of deferential wife and servant. Again, this scere is highly contrived. The center ground is dominated by a framed silhouette, reminiscent of the pseudo-ancestors in the last picture, and again, I would propose that this picture is designed to deceive; for at a time when Schwitters was coming under ferocious attack from his critics for his Merz pictures and poems, this photo was almost certainly taken to demonstrate to the public that the press was unjustified in damning him as a crazed Bolshevist revolutionary. In photos of Schwitters' home in Waldhausenstrasse 5 in Hanover, we may again perceive the gesture of concealment behind the costly ornamental facade. In fact at least five families lived in this house—six during the early 1920s—and as Schwitters' own apartment was too small to accommodate a studio, he had no choice but to work in the little space available to him in the ground floor apartment of his parents. Bruno Taut once noted that the Wilhelmine facade was like a wolf in sheep's clothing, and it is worth remembering that in 1919 it was behind those conventional net curtains on the second floor that Schwitters was composing the explosive arena of the Merz stage, with its defiant claims to unlimited space.

An early sculptural assemblage entitled *Die Heilige Bekümmernis* was also created in Waldhausenstrasse, and was one of the few Merz works with which Schwitters had himself photographed. There have been many interpretations of this assemblage (which was later incorporated into the Merzbau) as a bitter comment on the revolutionary Germany of 1919, but most analyses are

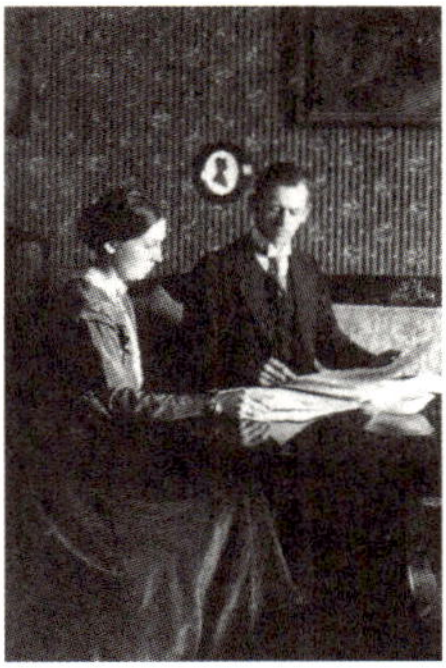 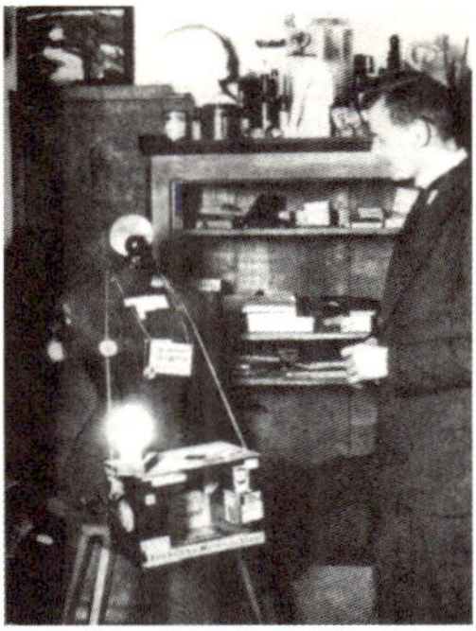

Helma and Kurt Schwitters in the Biedermeier room, Waldhausenstr. 5, Hanover 1919

Kurt Schwitters in front of *Die Heilige Bekümmernis*, about 1920

confined to the dummy figure, and omit the rest of the picture. This work, however, was not destined for a museum or gallery, but was evidently designed to be seen with the artist, and in a particular context. Gone are the genteel furnishings and formal polished surroundings; the figure stands left, the artist to the right, so that the central focus is on a well-lit pile of oddments stuffed into a far from elegant bookcase bearing a miscellaneous collection of old bottles, cans, and brushes. Here we are confronted by a photograph that presents us with a complex network of gestures deriving from a kind of ménage à trios, in which materials function as the unifying element between artist and work. Schwitters not only used his mother's tailor's dummy hung about with refuse to provide a commentary on the very foundations of life in Germany, but has also appropriated the domestic environment to display his construction. This photograph seems to me to represent a defining moment in Schwitters' career; this is art informed entirely by its prosaic surroundings, far removed from any aesthetic context. The figure, which was never exhibited and apparently was later absorbed in the Merzbau, provides a critique of post-1918 society, and the artist leaves it in the most unwelcome place possible—in the leafy suburbs, the very place where people do not want to know about the brutal injustices of the German revolution. This is not only a figure that presents a challenge to or a protest against its environment; unnervingly, it is its environment.

Schwitters' may have changed his personal image in the 1920s, discarding the Prussian gesture implicit in the high stiff Vatermörder collar, moustache, and stern gaze in favor of a more relaxed demeanor, but he chose to maintain the new look in the old setting of bourgeois Hanover, a phenomenon that most of his friends remarked on with wonder at some time. In Richard Huelsenbeck's assessment of the disagreements between Berlin Dada and Schwitters, it was in part Schwitters' attitude to space that branded him as a heretic in Dada's eyes. "I visited Schwitters shortly before Christmas," Huelsenbeck wrote in later years, "and the tree was already standing decorated in the living room. Frau Schwitters was bathing her son in a huge old-fashioned bath. We, who regarded the desert, the military barracks, the empty room, as the best place to be in, couldn't stop ridiculing Schwitters. Here, for us, was the German forest and a bench with hearts carved on it." Yet Schwitters' accomplishments in terms of space were, ironically, pure Dada, a clear rejection of the intellectual, hierarchical culture machine mediating between aesthetics and daily life. It became Schwitters' strategic gesture to make his collages and recite his poems in private houses, on beaches, in cafes, and on trains, in fact wherever he went, and from 1924 he made further advances into the public domain with his Merz advertising agency and Merz magazine. When Schwitters carved out a space for himself in the suburbs of staid, middle-class Hanover, it was with the freedom of those scurrilous Shakespearean figures who are permitted to speak the truth simply because they adopt the gestures of the fool. Szeemann reminds us of the entry in the Steinitz guest book in which Schwitters refers to himself as "Bürger and Idiot," citizen and idiot—and not even a citizen of trendy, cosmopolitan Berlin, but of embarrassingly provincial, tediously respectable Hanover, which preferred to confine culture to places where one recognized it as culture, and where it was available only for those who could afford it.

From the start, the Merzbau was located in Schwitters' house in Waldhausenstrasse. To integrate art into a domestic setting was unusual, but not unprecedented. In the early 1920s, the contemporary art exhibitions of Hanover's prestigious Galerie von Garvens were situated in the Garvens family home, while across the Atlantic,

Schwitters' patron Katherine Dreier used a selection of conservative furniture from department stores to furnish four rooms of an exhibition space like a little apartment, where she hung collages by Schwitters' and works by Arp, to demonstrate that modern art should and could be integrated into the average household. Richard Strauss created a more lasting monument to the domestic in art—and something of a scandal—with his *Sinfonia Domestica*, a self-portrait of Mr and Mrs Strauss at home, featuring the parents fussing over a screaming baby, visits from fond uncles and aunts, and occasional outbursts from Strauss' notoriously temperamental wife, Pauline. The composer's ultimate scandalous gesture was to premiere the symphony in a department store in New York (remembering that such stores often had Jewish owners and, particularly in Germany, were subject to anti-Semitic propaganda). Today the *Sinfonia Domestica* has been safely removed to the concert hall, but the Merzbau was an integral part of Waldhausenstrasse 5 and, at least in its later stages, largely immovable. When Alfred Barr, the director of The Museum of Modern Art in New York, arrived at Schwitters' home to inspect the Merzbau, he was aghast—how, he asked, did the artist intend to display it? The answer was, one had to knock at the front door of

Waldhausenstrasse, be assaulted (as contemporaries often related) by the smell of cooking cabbage, glue, and guinea pigs, be received by Schwitters' parents, and walk along the corridor to the rooms at the back, inspect the Merzbau and then bid a polite farewell to Herr and Frau Schwitters, remembering that they had no understanding for Merz: Eduard Schwitters was especially aggressive regarding his son's art. Even Schwitters' angelic wife Helma referred to his behavior as "tyrannical." Eduard died in 1931, but one wonders if he ever knew that his son was constructing something he called the Cathedral of Erotic Misery in one of his back rooms—in Szeemann's words, creating a remarkable *freie Ehe*, a cohabitation, between the world of art and the everyday environment, in a space that was very limited, often inhospitable, and in addition not even Schwitters' own.

This alternative name that art historians often assign to the Merzbau, the KdeE (Cathedral of Erotic Misery), was in fact rarely used by Schwitters; it occurs only in a few photographs of 1928 and in the "Veilchenheft" (Merz 21) issue of his Merz magazine. The very word "cathedral", of course, evokes the classical image of the Gesamtkunstwerk, particularly as understood by Expressionists in the early 1920s (we remember

Feininger's woodcut of the Cathedral for the 1919 Bauhaus manifesto), but Schwitters is circumspect in his use of the word.

"It is called the Cathedral of Erotic Misery or KdeE for short—we live in a time of abbreviations. The name KdeE is only a name. It relates to nothing of the content ... as the column has taken seven years to construct, the form has developed increasingly strictly, especially in the ribs, in keeping with my continuing spiritual development. The overall impression is now more or less reminiscent of Cubist painting or Gothic architecture (not one bit!)."

Szeemann reminds us here of another typical Schwitters gesture—to score an own-goal at crucial moments. Yes, we read, this is called a cathedral, but actually it isn't, not with regard to the content, though the form is Gothic—but then again, it isn't. This is less a text on the Merzbau than a game played with the reader; from other sources we know that at this time Schwitters' studio was expanding into a kind of multi-purpose environment. It served not only as a workplace but also as a theater in which he recited his poems, a gallery in which he exhibited his own collection of pictures "to provide guidance to the latest in art" and a showpiece for others' contributions (Hannah Höch, Lissitsky, Moholy Nagy, Gabo, Vordemberge-Gildewart, and possibly others created constructions in the Merzbau). It was also to become his bedroom and library, and into this work, which art historians so often describe as a sanctuary, he even incorporated kitsch and accepted the ideas of amateurs such as the Dutch Mathematics professor, who suggested he structure the floor.

It is hardly surprising that this unprecedented creation persuaded Carola Giedion-Welcker that here indeed was an attempt to create a Gesamtkunstwerk. In his book on the Merzbau, however, Dietmar Elger reminds us that Schwitters never referred to his masterpiece as a total work of art. In fact Schwitters does not refer to the Merzbau at all until 1930, and even then he only mentions columns in passing in a private letter. The word "Merzbau" itself is not used until 1933, and even after that only for official publications: the term does not occur in his private correspondence until after he has emigrated to Norway; to the end of his life (as in my introductory quote) Schwitters inexplicably preferred to use the word studio, although by the late 1930s the Merzbau extended to several rooms of his house. Now if we take Schwitters at his word, perhaps we should be not be thinking of the

Merzbau in a conventional art-historical manner, but in quite different terms. I would like to suggest that in the Merzbau Schwitters was not negotiating the boundaries of what we understand as a work of art, but rather negotiating the boundaries of what we understand as a studio; that is, the space between the artist and the world outside.

I would like to draw a parallel here between Schwitters' studio and what the great art historian Aby Warburg referred to as the "Denkraum," which can (rather inadequately) be translated as "thought space." Warburg conceived of the Denkraum as a kind of buffer zone in which the human being translates the demands and threats of the chaotic external world into comprehensible forms and gestures—a personal space of contemplation that houses the processes of interpretation (one is reminded of Wordsworth's "emotion recollected in tranquility.") An important aspect of Warburg's Denkraum is that it is not static and displays no linearity from chaos to order, but is an interference process, possessing a rhythm, a circulation that always has to be recognized, reflected, and experienced anew. Warburg gave material expression to his Denkraum in his extraordinary library, which was moved from Hamburg to London in the 1930s.

This was not a library in the conventional sense, but a far more dynamic invention: when new books were added, it would change the constellation of any one section, and Warburg would often shift books to other parts of the library and reclassify them as a result of the new emphasis. (A brief glance at the library's Internet site [www.welib.de] shows that the basis of Warburg's unorthodox categories has been maintained to this day.)

Warburg's life and work are in many ways comparable to those of Schwitters. Both were particularly vulnerable figures, Warburg because he was Jewish, Schwitters because of his epilepsy, a condition for which there was virtually no treatment at this time. (Sufferers were often deemed psychotic and confined to psychiatric institutions, and during the Third Reich were compulsorily sterilized.) Both Schwitters and Warburg were concerned with projects that confronted intolerance and prejudice head-on, and both were concerned to dispense with what Warburg called the "border control of disciplines"—his interest as an art historian was in the image as such, whether on a Botticelli painting or a postage stamp. It is worth mentioning here that idiosyncratic figures such as Schwitters and Warburg were possibly more in need of a

Denkraum than most, for those who dismissed the prevalent discourses in the Weimar Republic were liable to encounter fierce public resistance. Weimar artists and intellectuals are often portrayed as working in some sort of aesthetic vacuum, and it is easy to forget the opposition faced by the avant-garde—the extraordinary antagonism aroused by the Bauhaus throughout its existence, for instance, the sacking of museum directors for purchasing works by Schwitters and his colleagues, and the everlasting attempts to equate avant-garde art with insanity by prominent academics who should have known better.

In later life, Warburg mourned what he saw as the loss of the Denkraum in Weimar culture with the introduction of space-conquering techniques that seemed erode any possibility for reflection. Where this was to lead was not even evident to Szeemann when in 1974 he talked about the unrealizable Gesamtkunstwerk; he could not have foreseen the digital revolution that was to render the traditional forms of media almost indistinguishable, and which a quarter of a century later led Rosalind Krauss in her essay "Reinventing the Medium" to plead for a return to the idea of the medium as such, in order, as she wrote, "to reclaim the specific from the deadening embrace of the general." One wonders how Warburg would have reacted to reality TV, and whether he and Schwitters, if they had lived in our time, would have been among the first bloggers, the first to create a new kind of Denkraum between themselves and the might of the electronic media.

As the zone between an antagonistic outside world and Schwitters' Merz art, we may consider his studio in terms of a spatial Denkraum in which his turbulent age was explored and structures formulated. The more Schwitters collapsed the space between art and life, the more we may postulate the need for a Denkraum through which his impressions were filtered, examined, evaluated, and re-evaluated. From descriptions of the studio in the early 1920s, this was a place where visitors found themselves knee-deep in junk; it was here that Schwitters piled up discarded material, in this intermediate thought space between himself and a threatening world that started just down the corridor in his parents' apartment. It is as if Schwitters was desperately trying to make sense of a chaotic post-1918 Germany, with its roller-coaster currency, see-saw politics, blurred genders, and the advent of the swastika, adopted as an insignia in 1920 by a former army corporal whom his followers called the Führer.

At first Schwitters formed this material into columns, silent gestures in themselves; they can never be seen all at once and their interior contains some highly enigmatic material. It was not until he gained public acceptance in the late 1920s and early 1930s, and made inroads into the urban environment with his advertising agency and his architectural and typographical projects, that the studio constructions were transformed into a far more confident and flowing creation. This may provide a clue as to why Schwitters saw no need to make reference to his studio constructions in the 1920s; perhaps it was only when he realized that this place of transition was more representative of the Merz idea than any finished work, that he began to focus on it as a medium in itself, for which no other word was available apart from that of "studio." What started life as an intermediate space at some point in the 1920s, began to take on a life of its own and was finally envisaged as a new kind of community space, like Walter Benjamin's Paris arcades or Siegfried Kracauer's hotel lobby.

I have represented the Merzbau here as an example of the Hang zum Gesamtkunstwerk in the positive sense envisaged by Harald Szeemann, that is, as a "poetic zone of thought constructions" that becomes increasingly inclusive as it develops. In an essay of 1997, however, Dorothea Dietrich interpreted the Merzbau not as an embracing of the environment, but rather as an effort to sidestep it or mask its potential menace. Ultimately, she depicts Schwitters' Merzbau as an attempt to heal the experience of rupture that confronted him in the unstable world of the Weimar Republic. She describes the grottoes of the Merzbau as resonating with the rhetoric of Germany's conservatives and claims that his use of equilibrium "is weighted toward the organic ... and reveals the fundamentally conservative tenor of his art. If not a precursor of the Nazis, Schwitters [and the reactionary modernists] must be regarded as facilitators. Supporting and contributing to a world image shaped by irrationality, they helped create an atmosphere of anti-reason that made the growth of Nazi ideology possible."

Apart from the fact that Dietrich bases this sweeping judgment of the Merzbau on its presumed organic form and the content of a few grottoes made in 1923, this statement seems to me to be a misrepresentation of the Merz discourse. Schwitters was never lost or overcome by his urban civilization as the Expressionists were; it was the subject of his art, and the very name Merz was taken from the world of commerce. Everything Schwitters includes in his art passes through the studio that is also his Denkraum, and all the material selected for inclusion in Merz is first scrutinized for its ambivalence, then set in a further context of paradox and contradiction. In the end, we are never allowed to see the final product all at once; as with his columns, one has, so to speak, to walk around Schwitters' Merz works and view them from all sides, and Schwitters deliberately sets out to prevent them being pinned down to any single agenda.

The key terms that Dietrich employs in her accusation that Merz paved the way for the Third Reich are "organic" and "irrational." I would, however, like to suggest that it was not the desire for the organic or the irrational that led to the rise of National Socialism, but the desire for hierarchy, for the authoritarian gesture, and as we have seen, Schwitters neatly circumvents all hierarchical discourses of his time, both by his use of material and, wherever possible, by locating his art outside any conventional setting. Other of his contemporaries adopted similar tactics by turning their attention to human activities that society regarded as worthless, or that could not be categorized within any dominant discourse. Freud collated his patients' dreams, Hans Prinzhorn examined the artistic skills of his schizophrenic patients, Eric Satie listed bottles and other household articles to be used as orchestral instruments for the ballet *Parade*, Bartok traveled extensively to record the elemental language of unnotated folk music. As for the rational discourse of the 1920s, the alternative model to Dietrich's irrational and organic world image, it is here, if anywhere, that we find evidence of the authoritarian discourse, particularly in those architectural projects of the age that expressly avoided entering into a dialogue with residents or the environment. Le Corbusier abhored the street and was never a supporter of democracy, and his suggestions in the 1930s for the wholesale reconstruction of major European cities such as Paris ran parallel to the ambitious building program of the NSDAP that from 1933 was implemented throughout Germany's towns and cities with extraordinary speed. Le Corbusier wrote that his aim was "to clear away from our cities the dead bones that putrefy in them"; it was left to Schwitters to incorporate the rejected dead bones into his work, a prime example being the Molde grotto incorporated into the Merzbau in 1935.

Schwitters was highly involved in the world of the new architecture, of course; working for and with leading architects of his time such as Walter Gropius and Mies van der Rohe, but he also voiced criticism of the lack of interest in concepts of integration of old and new, of architecture and its location—the kind of attitude that led Mies van der Rohe to declare in 1924, "Architecture is the will of the age, nothing else ... The tendency of our time is wholly oriented toward the secular ... We will build no cathedrals ... The individual declines increasingly in significance: his fate no longer interests us." Schwitters' approach to such dogma was invariably subversive rather than antagonistic. In 1927, for instance, the gestures implied in Mies van der Rohe's vast doorways became the target of typical Schwitterian irony:

> I can't imagine that you can simply walk through Mies van der Rohe's doors, rather you stride through them. Great noble beings stride through these doors, full of a new spirit. But it can turn out that, as on the Frankfurt housing estates, people move in with their green plush sofas. It can turn out in the end that the residents are not so mature or liberated as their own doors. We'll just have to hope the house will turn them into noble beings ...

Harald Szeemann portrayed Schwitters' struggle with ideologies as not only subversive, but subversively heroic. Although the later stages of the Merzbau are often described as Constructivist, Szeemann maintains that they are better described as a manual of Constructivist misuse, and he leaves us with a final gesture by Schwitters, who, like a mythological hero, twists the arm of the right angle and forces it to the ground in a trial of strength. Carola Giedion-Welcker saw Schwitters rather differently, as a latter-day Laocoön whose Merzbau echoed Laocoön's last cry, "O my poor people, Men of Troy, what madness has come over you?" As Giedion-Welcker, who visited Schwitters in 1935, was one of the last people to see the Hanover Merzbau before its destruction, I'd like to close with her portrayal of the Merzbau as Gesamtkunstwerk:

> One senses the years of inflation in which bank notes were devalued by the hour and piled up as useless rubbish. And it was also the time of hunger strikes, mass revolts, and social revolution in Germany. Kurt Schwitters captures just this atmosphere in creating a symbolic [mode of] expression. He does not describe, he does not narrate; he

suggests a general climate ... In calling himself Merz, Schwitters wanted to establish a final identity between work and artist, creator and creation. Schwitters dreamed of—and worked till the end of his life on—the realization of his Gesamtkunstwerk, the Merz column ... One senses how he unites clear-cut constructions with haphazard proliferations, and how often in these constructed reliefs transience—in effect the gnawing of time—is articulated by damaged material, scoured and washed ashore by the sea, rusted in the damp, or spewed out by the metropolis. 'Weathering—Schwittering' (Verwitterung—Verschwitterung), as he once said, to give things their inner luster, their tragic beauty, their patina, the incursion of time, a sign of the transitory nature of all that exists. This is apparent even in his Merz column, whose compact construction he suddenly intersperses with caves and niches, with unconstrained branchings, in order to integrate a visual rendering of his poetic fancies, those allusions to Germany's fossilized pillars of learning and its proliferation of mystic utopias, which he discerned well before they broke out in catastrophic mass hysteria. This too is a "colonne sans fin", not as a prayer ascending to heaven like that of Brancusi, but a sign of the times with infinite reverberations, one that for him never ceases as long as life lasts and also as long as his life lasted.

Appendix: Processed

Roger Cardinal, "The Hanover Merzbau: Tracing a Lost Masterwork," in Louise Edson (ed.), *Conjunctions, Verbal-Visual Relations*, San Diego 1996.

Peter Bissegger, "The Reconstruction of Kurt Schwitters' Merzbau," http://merzbaurekonstruktion.com/

Dorothea Dietrich, "Merz and the Longing for Wholeness," in: Charlotte Stokes and Stephen C. Foster (ed.), *Dada Cologne Hanover: Crisis and the Arts, The History of Dada*, vol 3, G.K. Hall & Co, New York 1997, p. 109–135.

Karel Dudesek, *Virtual reality—3D version of the Merzbau*, a project by Zvonimir Bakotin. Interactive 3D (VRML) model of Merzbau [http://www.merzbau.org] is part of the content for VMS—Virtual Museum System [http://www.kurt-schwiters.org].

John Elderfield, *Kurt Schwitters*, Thames and Hudson, London 1985.

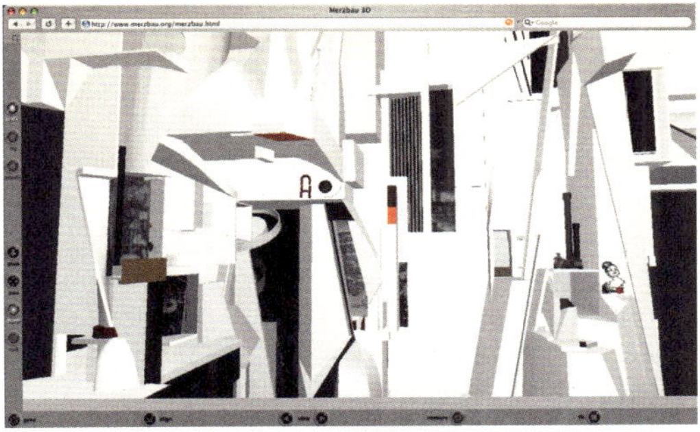

Screenshot from *Virtual reality—3D version of the Merzbau*, a project by Zvonimir Bakotin, interactive 3D (VRML) model of Merzbau [http://www.merzbau.org]

Dietmar Elger, *Der Merzbau von Kurt Schwitters. Eine Werkmonographie*, Kunstwissenschaftliche Bibliothek, vol. 12, Verlag der Buchhandlung Walther König, Cologne 1984 (1999).

Curt Germundson, "Kurt Schwitters and the Alternative Art Community in Hanover," in: Stokes and Foster (ed.), *Dada Cologne Hanover*, p. 206–231.

Carola Giedion-Welcker, "Kurt Schwitters. Gesamtausstellung in Hannover," *Baseler Nationalzeitung*, February 16, 1956.

Carola Giedion-Welcker, "Hans Arp und Kurt Schwitters, Zu einer Doppelausstellung" and "Kurt Schwitters. Konstruktive Metamorphose des Chaos," in: Carola Giedion-Welcker, *Gesammelte Schriften 1926–1971*, Dumont Verlag, Cologne 1973, p. 277–284; 285–288.

Annja Müller-Alsbach and Heinz Stahlhut, *Kurt Schwitters. Merz – ein Gesamtweltbild*, exh. cat., Museum Tinguely, Basel & Bern 2004. Concept by Annja Müller-Alsbach and Heinz Stahlhut. With contributions by: Guido Magnaguagno, "Foreword," p. 9–18; Iris Bruderer-Oswald, "The New Optics. Kurt Schwitters, Carola Giedion-Welcker and Sigfried Giedion," p. 22–31; Karin Orchard, "Kurt Schwitters's Spatial Growths," p. 32–49; Peter Bissegger, "Notes on the Reconstruction of the Merzbau," p. 66–67; Eric Hattan, "Merzbauafter-merz," p. 68; Eric Hattan, "Anarchistic Proliferation—Safe and Secure," p.70; Beat Wyss, "Merzpicture Horse Grease. Art in the Age of Mechanical Reproduction," p. 72–84; Jakob Kolding, "Contesting Architecture and Social Space," p. 86–87; Daniel Spoerri, "Nine written questions about Kurt Schwitters," p. 88–92; Christoph Bignens, "Cogs and Wheels," p. 108–119; Kurt Schwitters, "The Raddadist Machine," p. 120; Konrad Klapheck, "The Maschine and I," p. 122; Ralf Burmeister, "'Related Opposites.' Difference in Mentality between Dada and Merz," p. 140–149; Klaus Staeck, "For Me There is No Such Thing as Unpolitical Art," p. 150; Thomas Hirschhorn, "Dada is important to me," p. 152; Christian Janecke, "Schwitters and Chance," p. 168–179; Jean Tinguely, "The Brazilian Baked Apple Tube," p. 200–203; Juri Steiner, "The Tale of Paradise Dada, Merz and the 'Other' Oeuvre," p. 208–215; Karl Gerstner, "Kurt Schwitters: A Virtual Reminiscence," p. 216–217.

Kurt Schwitters Archiv in the Sprengel Museum Hanover: http://www.schwitters.info.

Beatrix Nobis, *Kurt Schwitters und die romantische Ironie*, VDG, Alfter 1993.

Ernst Nündel, *Kurt Schwitters*, Rowohlt Verlag, Hamburg 1981.

Karin Orchard & Isabel Schulz (ed.), *Kurt Schwitters Catalogue Raisonné 1923–36*, Hatje Cantz Verlag, Ostfildern 2003.

Cornelia Osswald-Hoffmann, *Zauber- und Zeigeräume, Raumgestaltung der 20er und 30er Jahre*, Akademischer Verlag, Munich 2003.

Werner Schmalenbach, *Kurt Schwitters*, DuMont-Schauberg, Cologne, 1967.

Kurt Schwitters: Die neue Gestaltung der Typographie, printed privately, Werbebroschüre, Hanover o. J. (um 1925), reprinted in Lach 1975.

Harald Szeemann, "Zum Gesamtkunstwerk von Kurt Schwitters," *Zeitlos auf Zeit*, Lindinger + Schmid Verlag, Regensburg 1994.

Frühlicht, vol. I, magazine 3, ed. Bruno Taut, Magdeburg 1922 (Schloß und Kathedrale mit Hofbrunnen, 1920/1922, p. 87).

Gwendolen Webster, *Kurt Merz Schwitters*, University of Wales Press, Cardiff 1997.

Gwendolen Webster, "Kurt Schwitters and Katherine Dreier," *German Life and Letters*, vol. 52, no. 4, October 1999, p. 443–456.

Lambert Wiesing, *Stil statt Wahrheit*, Verlag Wilhelm Fink, Munich 1991.

Sarah Wilson, "Kurt Schwitters en Angleterre," *Kurt Schwitters*, exh. cat., Centre Georges Pompidou, Paris 1994.

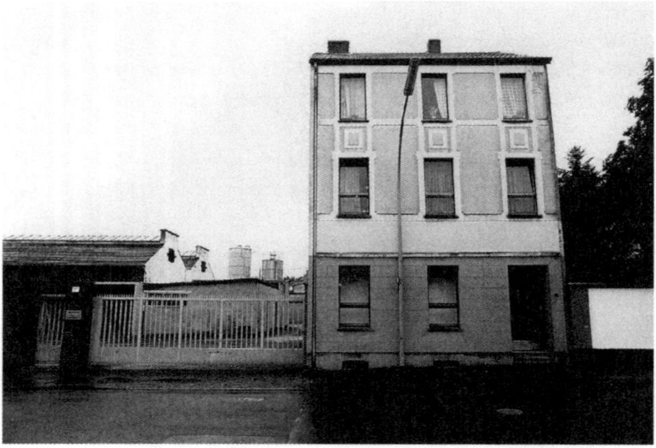

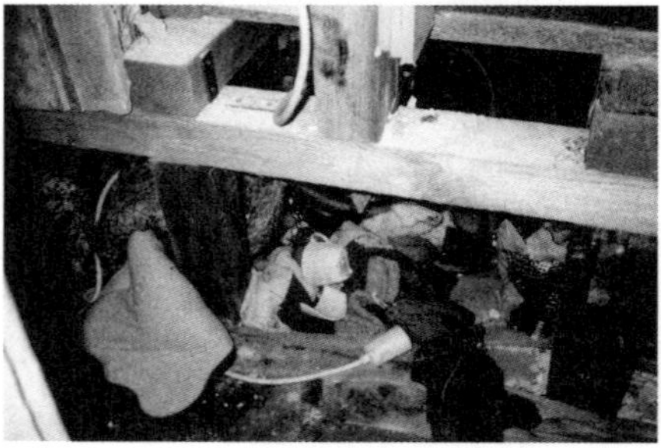

GREGOR SCHNEIDER *house u r*, Rheydt 1985–2000

Chapter Two: Processing

"The house is past."[1]

Kurt Schwitters and Gregor Schneider

Karin Orchard

The Merzbau assembled by Kurt Schwitters (1887–1948) in Hanover remains one of the iconic early works of installation art, even though it was destroyed in 1943. However, it was not unique in kind. One has to pass through several European countries to follow the sequence of the respectively bombed, burnt-down, collapsed, or incomplete volume-enclosing structures that Schwitters persevered in building in every succeeding location that had to become his home. His various Merzbauten and associated structures—in Hanover, in Lysaker (near Oslo), on the Norwegian islet of Hjertøya, in the British internment camp on the Isle of Man, and in Elterwater in the Lake District—are all essentially a continuation in geographically and chronologically discrete installments of one and the same original work, restarted over and over again from the beginning of the 1920s, and evolving stylistically throughout its creator's life.

The Schwitters microcosm which is the Merzbau functions as a time capsule and space capsule inside which historical events, memories, and his entire life are recorded. The Merzbau is flexible, being itself fixed neither in time nor in space, so that Schwitters' private feelings and historical experiences can repeatedly re-adjust to the temporal dimensions of past and present, and to the changes in location. This is architecture on a human scale, strongly individualized to become a shell housing private memories: a mind structure. Palimpsest-fashion, different periods intermingle and overlie each other within a memory and image store, ramifying outward, network-like, to different locations. If one considers the various Merzbauten in terms of the "distributed network" concept, and at the same time analyzes their functions, the use made of them, and in particular the role played by Kurt Schwitters himself as a live component of his constructions, it becomes clear that this early avant-garde, space-enclosing project can be regarded as a precursor of the present-day artistic activities which have been carried on for some years past under such names as concept mapping, LKW (for *Lebenskunstwerk*) (Life as

Artwork), performance installation, or *soziale Praxis* (social interaction).

Gregor Schneider, born in 1969, is one of the most single-minded and radical representatives of this younger generation. Looking at how Schneider handles and creates space, one might well assume at first glance that he has a great deal in common with Kurt Schwitters and the Merzbau. However, any close analysis of Schneider's creative work as a whole since 1985 will inevitably show that the similarities are purely superficial.

Like Kurt Schwitters, Gregor Schneider took over a multi-occupation, several-storey residential building owned by his parents. The 16-year-old son needed a studio. The building in question, vacant at the time, was in the town of Rheydt, in Unterheydener Strasse, next to the premises occupied by his father's lead-processing business. From 1985 to 2001, Gregor Schneider worked in this *Haus u r*, as he called it—worked in it and worked on it: he built new conventional rooms into the existing conventional rooms, put walls in front of walls, suspended new ceilings, walled up doorways, constructed windows in front of other windows; a warped house shape dangles, inverted, from the ceiling, corridors narrow progressively, some of the rooms can be reached only by crawling through narrow passageways and adits closed off by grilles, one room is mounted on rollers and can rotate on its own axis, the top of an ordinary ladder emerging from a hatch in the floor invites the visitor to explore the rooms that lie below—these lined with sound-deadening polystyrene—and some rooms have extraordinary thicknesses of insulating material—itself of the most diverse kinds—resulting in walls and doors of several times the normal thickness.

The title *u r*, though taken from the street address of Unterheydener Strasse, Rheydt, stands for *umbauter Raum* (room built around space). Numbered consecutively, the rooms built around space mark intermediate stages in the work program. At first glance, looking at these rooms, walls, ceilings, and floors, one does not immediately notice that they have been changed; they look like entirely commonplace, run-of-the-mill rooms such as would be found in any home, rather spartanly furnished, certainly, but otherwise entirely unremarkable. The invisibility of the work done is part of Schneider's artistic strategy. It takes a schooled observer to spot what is not normal: a ceiling that is too low, an excessively narrow connecting passage, steps leading nowhere, strangely dead acoustics, for instance, in the windowless *u r 12, Total Isoliertes*

Gästezimmer u r 12 (*Totally Insulated Guest Room*, 1995). As a result of 16 years of continuous rebuilding—incidentally just about the same length of time that Kurt Schwitters had for working on his first Merzbau in Hanover—Gregor Schneider is no longer in a position to supply plans or elevations for any part of *Haus u r* itself. His own record of the changes made has lacunae and blind spots; his house has become a place strange to him. Externally, as with the Merzbau, the house has not changed: all the rebuilding work is carried on within its walls, and the house can only be explored from inside. Normal installations such as water, heating, and electricity are either non-functional or only partly functional. In some of the rooms, lighting and fans are used to simulate times of day—a feature that Schwitters had used earlier. In spite of all this, the house remained up until very recently the place where Gregor Schneider lived and worked. It also remained a "private" house at all times, never becoming a place of public exhibition or an art center—though Schneider did invite selected art critics and curators to come and see it, and evidently adhered to a fixed tour of inspection when he conducted them round the house and provided his commentary.

Schneider's involvement in art goes back to pubescent years, at which time he experimented with extreme situations and "performance"-type stunts: he buried himself in a hole in the ground, swung around overarm through trees, coated his body in flour-and-water paste, visited the exact spot where a female art student had been murdered. In 1986 he constructed two identical, perfectly insulated crates. He was interested in whether it would be possible to detect which crate had a person concealed inside. From here it was not a big step to the rooms built around the space of *Haus u r*. "At the start, the rooms were simply expanded boxes."[2]

Can one really determine whether the wall conceals a further wall behind it, or whether this second wall is built of red brick or pale brick? What generates the sense of unease that is felt in some of the rooms? Is it what one knows of Gregor Schneider's way of operating and of his construction techniques, or is it the remarks that he occasionally lets drop on the subject of the uncanny? As he conducts visitors round the house, Schneider keeps subtly feeding their fears—fears of being lost in the house, of a door closing behind one and leaving no way out, of a cry for help—or scream—in the insulated, soundproofed rooms being quite inaudible outside them, ultimately the fear that one has walked into a trap set by a psychopath. The unexpected discoveries to which he subjects the house's visitors are clichés like the body in the cellar or the unsecured trapdoor. This strategy of steering and influencing the recipient is part of his concept. There is in fact a considerable danger that Schneider will be identified with his work: that people will be quick to read it as self-revelation, as a voyage through a psychopathic inner life. Recognizing this, he prudently shuns publicity and media exposure, and attends exhibition openings, if at all, only as an (absentee) performer.

"THE ROOM DOES NOT INTEREST ME IN THE LEAST"

It soon becomes clear that Schneider's primary concern is not with the formal or aesthetic aspects of designing rooms in either the sculptural or the architectural sense. Nor—in this he is like Schwitters—does he have a final, definitive design aim in mind; the nature of his work is continual process, so all is subject to change. Gregor Schneider may assert: "The room does not interest me in the least,"[3] yet it is of course "rooms" and their atmospheres that he creates, even if all they represent for him personally is a mere set of side-effects generated as he pursues his real aim.

As he works on *Haus u r*, he is primarily interested in—indeed, obsessed by—the process character of "working" as such, fascinated by an activity which potentially could achieve autonomous reality to the point of uncontrollability: he could "simply carry on working until the work kicks me out of the house or swallows me whole."[4] "It's still about work I have to do but can't *know* any longer [...] it's about work making you forgotten."[5] For Schneider, "Action is a higher form than thought"; he is interested in the "self-perpetuating momentum of action,"[6] the very process of consuming working energy by unceasingly rebuilding, dismantling, reinstalling: "That was brutal work, it killed the economy stone dead."[7] The crucial requirement for him is that changes, moods, feelings, emotions should be registered, yet without any cause for them being either apparent or even amenable to rational enquiry. "Movement that cannot be consciously perceived (like that of the rotatable coffee room or the variable-height ceiling), movement of things and the various times of day, generates—as I call it—an unknowable time-space. It creates a place that cannot exist as a place, an intuition of something we cannot know."[8] Schneider's room creations are really room destructions, undertaken with the aim of attaining to knowledge at a higher level. The key points are the differing states that the rooms are found in, their atmospheres as determined by their contingent nature, their circumstances and time-spaces. The *Total Isoliertes Gästezimmer* has a quite different impact in Paris, compared with its impact in Rheydt or in Venice. Why this should be is impossible to determine. Is it a matter of constructional differences, which cannot be appreciated at first glance? Or does the answer lie in the different frames of mind of a given visitor at different times? And anyway, how many visitors consciously perceive what differences and what mood changes?

DUPLICATION

The house goes public: at various times since 1994, for exhibition purposes, particular rooms have been removed, entire or in sections, and reinstalled in the house after the end of the exhibition concerned; replicas were produced of certain rooms—for instance the *Liebeslaube* (*Lovers' Bower*, 2000)—for the Sprengel Museum in Hanover, and these either remained on display or were sold to collectors, the original room meanwhile continuing to lead a parallel existence in *Haus u r*. These secondments of individual rooms, and of the entire house in the case of the Venice Biennale in 2001, have been referred to by Schneider ever since as the *Totes Haus u r*

(*Dead House u r*). Even some exhibition arrangements outside the house at Rheydt are now duplicated, an example being the Bremerhaven exhibition entitled *u r 28. Müllsack in Wichsecke* (*u r 28. Rubbish Sack at Wank Corner*, 1999), which was repeated at the Kunsthalle in Hamburg in 2003, complete in all details including the exact room layout of the Bremerhaven Kabinett für aktuelle Kunst. It is disturbing to feel that nothing is simply identical with itself, that there is no such thing as completion, that everything is work-in-progress, everything is in flux, and that there is no way to anchor the work or the rooms spatially, no way to grasp them definitively.

The duplicated rooms function as full-size models: they are reproductions of reality created to mirror what is familiar and thereby expose or transform it. They are not theatrical illusions of rooms, but potential rooms. Gregor Schneider often uses hypothetical language. In 1989–1991, for example, in an empty house in Giesenkirchen—near Rheydt—he constructed a *Totally Insulated Death Room*, the insulation of which was literally measured in meters. He describes this room in the following terms: "This piece was not planned as a room experience, though one certainly felt greatly increased pressure on the ears when one bent down into the black void, with no way of knowing how far down it went. With this piece, one would have had to decide to commit oneself. If one had in fact entered the room, the door would have slammed shut. There was then no way of opening the room from either inside or outside. The interest for me lay in the implications of eliminating all mediation. Once inside this room, one would have ceased to exist as an object of sensory perception [...] I did not go in."[9] The radicalism that prompts the construction of such atmospheric chambers of horrors behind a facade of normality simply cannot deliver its full impact anywhere except at the original location. In that sense, *Haus u r* was indeed "killed" when it was metamorphosed into *Totes Haus u r*. It became a trompe-l'œil, a theatrical prop, a place now opened to the general public. What happens meantime to the literally gutted house in Rheydt? What does the future hold for *Totes Haus u r*? What is to be done with the memories held by the house and/or its rooms, memories of its early history as a family home, or its subsequent history as an exhibit stared at by a mass public in Venice and in Los Angeles? All these duplications and mirror images throw up a whole series of uncertainties relating to identity and difference.

ZWISCHENRÄUME (GAPS IN-BETWEEN)

When a wall is built in front of another wall, the result, regardless of size and shape, is a *gap*. Gregor Schneider maintained that the gaps were "never an end in themselves, they just happened because new items were put in."[10] Nonetheless, he both photographed and filmed these chaotic, filthy spaces, and the litter and junk lying in them. The rooms behind sliding walls matter to him because they are intermediate stages, transitional zones between inside and outside: "That is the important wall where I put the behind-wall pictures or between-wall bricks, or sometimes I put myself behind it."[11] In Rheydt, the visitor has to go through these gaps to get to the next room. In most exhibitions this glimpse of backstage reality is withheld, but there are a few, for example in Paris or the *Steindamm* installation in Hamburg, which include the rear aspect of the rooms in the overall concept.

The chaotic between-rooms in *Haus u r* contrast vividly with some rooms which come across as absolutely cool and sterile—for instance the *Totally Insulated Guest Room* or the *Bedroom*. These sparsely furnished rooms have been planned to the last detail and thoroughly tidied, and thus are finished, killed off: in these rooms, time has stopped. In other rooms again, such as the *Wunderkammer* (*Chamber of Miracles*) or the *Atelier* (*Studio*), a meticulously planned and arranged chaos tempts the visitors by offering significant details calculated to start them following a trail. In comparison, the places between and under walls and floors appear positively lively. Here, a place is assigned to objects which have no place—or are granted no place—elsewhere, which were hidden away from view, such as an inflatable sex doll, a wrecked birdcage, soiled clothes, rubbish bags. Most notably in the video *Night. Haus u r, October 1996*, attention is directed to the neglected, unused room behind; a real tour de force, the film documents the enormous effort it costs even Gregor Schneider himself to visit these forgotten places and inspect them. The eerieness engendered is accentuated here by the over-loud sounds of the cameraman's breathing and movements. By being documented on video or by being shown to people in the exhibition context, this leftover space, which one is not supposed to be in, is given a local habitation and reality. What was suppressed or repressed, the part of the self made inaccessible, the uncanny lurking in the gaps, here becomes visible.

Gregor Schneider compares his house to an onion. In the successive layers, significant things, historical things, are deposited. Behind the window of the *Chamber of Miracles*, for instance, which opens only onto another window, in the gap thus created between the two, there hang photographs of Schneider's parents and grandmother. "For every room layer, one generation. I guess I can pupate here."[12]

ALTER EGO AND DOPPELGÄNGER

Gregor Schneider has already produced several post-pupal forms: 1990 saw the addition of a second name to the doorbell plate at the entrance to the building: *Hannelore Reuen*; and since 1998 there has been a further alter ego, this one named *N. Schmidt*. Seeking ways to avoid imposing any sort of definitive state on the house, Gregor Schneider invents stage props, alternative identities, house-sharers. "I could go on working under a different name. It's about getting away from your own identity as an artist so you can start thinking straight again."[13] The introduction of the role-players and alternative identities ensured that the space occupied now is clearly a theater stage.

It remained to be seen what form Gregor Schneider's work would take after the death of the *Haus u r* had been staged in Venice. One project was realized in the East End of London in autumn 2004: *Die Familie Schneider in London* (*The Schneider Family in London*). As long ago as 1996, Schneider had been fantasizing: "I dream of just taking the whole house with me and building it somewhere else. Then my father and mother would be living in it, the older relatives lying dead in the basement, brothers upstairs, and there would be women and men living all around nearby because they have no place else special to go. Then on a seat in the corner somewhere the big woman who is always making babies and chucking them out into the world. And I am in there somewhere, digging it all up again all the time."[14] This recent work is a culmination of all his themes and motifs. Schneider here took two adjoining typical English terraced houses, of identical construction and layout, and in them staged two identical tableaux vivants. Visitors have to telephone an art-events agency to book a tour. They are taken to the houses and given a door key. They are only allowed in one at a time, and they only get ten minutes per house. The fusty, abnormal atmosphere inside evidently hits every visitor at once, and overpoweringly. Associations of crime and violence are insidiously suggested to the mind. A smell of moldering decay emanates from the basement below, and on the way down there is a locked door behind which one seems to hear a child crying alone. Hidden behind a set of shelves in the basement is a secret room, with a soiled mattress on the floor. In the kitchen on the ground floor, a woman is manically washing dishes, an overheated room on the first floor has a small individual sitting on a chair, head in a plastic bag, fighting desperately for breath; the visitor gets a fright from his own reflection in an enormous wall mirror. The rooms have no windows, though on the outside there are windows—so once again, evidently, rooms have been surreptitiously built inside rooms. Behind a shower curtain a naked man is standing masturbating in the bath, his back to the visitor. A peephole built into the skylight gives a view of pornographic graffiti. The visitor feels like an invisible, spectral voyeur, because nothing he can say produces any reaction at all from the Schneider family. Then when he leaves the first house and goes into the second, a shock of a quite different nature is in store for him: the houses are not just structurally identical, but have identical twins of the actors going through the same compulsive movements, nails hammered into the very same spot on the wall, the same damp patch in the same place on the floor, and so on. But are the two houses in fact identical? Is there really not a difference? These questions receive no answer, as no one is allowed back into the doppelgänger house to ascertain the facts. And as one walks back along the street past all the other houses, one can't help wondering what might be going on inside these walls, and whether they too might not be masking hidden rooms, hidden scenes of casual horror.

Kurt Schwitters and his artistically conceived rooms fuse into a single entity: they are externalized pieces of his identity. However, his emigration meant that he had to take them abroad with him, as the snail carries its house, and reinstall them at each new place where he settled. In this way, several times over, he creates a new "home" for himself. He has a romantic, idealistic goal: an all-embracing "Merzgesamtweltbild" (Merz view of the world).

Gregor Schneider, in total contrast, works in his rooms as a stranger would, waiting for the house to "do" something with him, waiting for it to answer his existential questions about identity and difference, to show him places which no one can know. He too bases his work on the concept of "home," for it is after all his parental home in his native town that he is purveying. But the doppelgänger rooms and personal aliases bring him no answer. His postmodern self is unable to form a unified image of the world as a whole.

Notes

1. Theodor W. Adorno, "Minima Moralia. Reflexionen aus dem beschädigten Leben" (Reflections from a Damaged Life), *Gesammelte Schriften* (*Collected Works*), vol. 4, Suhrkamp, Frankfurt am Main 1980, p. 42.
2. "'Man baut, was man nicht mehr kennen kann,' Amine Haase sprach mit Gregor Schneider vor der Eröffnung vom *Toten Haus u r* in Venedig," ('One is building something one can no longer know.' Amine Haase interviews Gregor Schneider before the opening of *Dead House u r* in Venice), *Kunstforum* 156, 2001, p. 289–303, 300.
3. "' ... Ich schmeisse nichts weg, ich mache immer weiter ... ' Gregor Schneider und Ulrich Loock im Gespräch" ('I don't chuck anything away, I just keep on going,' Gregor Schneider and Ulrich Loock in conversation), *Gregor Schneider*, exh. cat., Kunsthalle Bern 1996, p. 19–57, 22.
4. Schneider/Loock, "Ich schmeisse nichts weg," p. 19.
5. Schneider/Haase, "Man baut," p. 303.
6. Schneider/Loock, "Ich schmeisse nichts weg," p. 22.
7. Ibid., p. 25.
8. Ibid., p. 22.
9. Ibid., p. 42.
10. Schneider/Haase, "Man baut," p. 292.
11. Schneider/Loock, "Ich schmeisse nichts weg," p. 46.
12. Ibid., p. 55.
13. Schneider/Haase, "Man baut," p. 298.
14. Schneider/Loock, "Ich schmeisse nichts weg," p. 55.

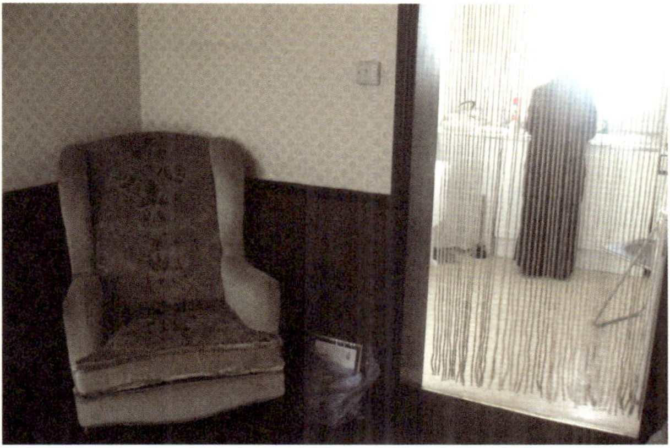

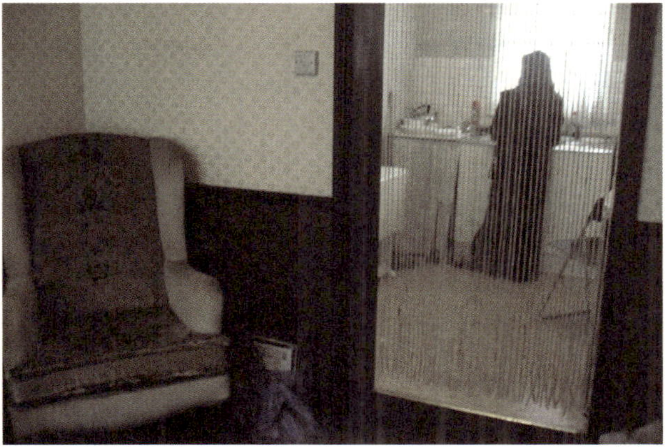

GREGOR SCHNEIDER *Die Familie Schneider in London, Waldenstreet 16*, 2004

GREGOR SCHNEIDER *Die Familie Schneider in London, Waldenstreet 14*, 2004

Merz World: Processing the Complicated Order

Yona Friedman in conversation
with Hans Ulrich Obrist

YONA FRIEDMAN What is most interesting for me in the Merzbau is what I would call a "Merz Principle." The Merz Principle means a random agglomeration of things that form a whole. I think this Merz Principle exists in everything. But first I have to clarify certain basic concepts: 1. Reality around us is not isolated facts, but rather processes. It is very important that it is not one part of the process that is interesting for us, but the process as a whole. The problem in particle physics is mathematical models. Mathematical models are absolutely perfect, except that they are unable to describe a process. They are conceived in order to give results. Now, in reality we are not really curious about the results except in engineering, for approximations, but we are interested in processes. A process can be described only and exclusively by its history, by a linear presentation. It means that we can have a different, less mathematical, and more precise presentation of the world around us by sequential description.

I sometimes use a very simple example: the space-time continuum is four-dimensional. In string theory it even goes from nine to 11 dimensions. And I pretend that we have a completely perfect, one-dimensional, linear description of the world: the DVD. The DVD gives you the presentation of a three-dimensional reality and of time. And it gives it simply by a very, very long sequence of 0s and 1s. These sequences are completely non-understandable. This means that we have a one-dimensional presentation of the physical world, a complete presentation, but it is not readable. It can be decoded but that is very, very difficult.

The second term that I use differently to the term of "complexity" is the term "complicated order." In complexity, extreme complexity, you have, for example, a finite number of elements; where there is a direct relation between all of them, there will be only a finite complexity, a finite number of elements. In the complicated order it is different. The complicated order is not a graph but a funny curve, which can go any way. Again: it is a one-dimensional relation, but for a finite number of elements I have infinite possible complicated orders. This is a very big difference. And what we meet is the complicated order. A characteristic of the complicated order is that you cannot make an abridged form through mathematical formulas. One such complicated order that we use everyday is alphabetical order.

We consider that it is an order, but there is no rule to it. The only rule is that we learnt it by heart when we were children. When I was in China I realized that it is absolutely not evident for the Chinese why c follows b. There is no explanation whatsoever. It is simply the way we learn it.

This complicated order is far more general than we think. My dog is a very intelligent being. He lives in a world where he is not using mathematical formulas at all, but he completely understands the world and shows absolutely healthy reactions. What I want to say is that you cannot describe behavior by mathematical formulae, except as sequences.

The difficulty with the city, with architectural products, is that they are based on behavior. Without the behavior of the user they are not complete. The only thing that completes them is that they are used. A building that has no user is not a building. It is a ruin. This shows that in architectural cities the planners are supposed to do something to satisfy the complicated order of behavior. But this is impossible because behavior is far more complicated than the DVD, and far more complicated than the alphabet. It is erratic. That means one step of somebody's behavior does not give us the slightest information about what will be its next step. It can be anything. I think that all this is in a way an explanation, the result for the Merzbau. For me, the Merzbau was one of the first objects to trigger this way of thinking. And we can say that it gets into every field. Therefore, I was saying, in a way jokingly, that we have a Merz principle and we live in a Merz world, in a world which is essentially erratic.

Intelligence starts with improvisation and this is true in every field. I have to be more precise about what I mean by improvisation. Many psychologists consider that we think in words but I think we don't think in words. We think in images. The word is only an abstraction to an image in the head. My daughter, for example, when she was four years old once said, "Oh, I see it in my head." This sort of image is a kind of improvisation. A good example is science: Newton and Einstein were improvisers. They had ideas born through improvisation. Only then was their work to find mathematical justification. So in this kind of work we improvise inside an erratic world and then, after that, we try to rationalize. And I think this is important as a principle because in classical architecture, in functionalist architecture, everywhere, it is first presented by the rational aspect. But it is in fact the rational aspect that should come afterwards.

First of all, it is an image—I don't like the word "vision"—that creative people build. They build this image and rationalize the theory after. For example, when I wrote my book *Realizable Utopias* (*Utopies réalisables*, L'éclat, Paris 2000) I started on this basis: first there is an unsatisfactory situation and you imagine a way to get out of it; once you have this image, you look for how to do it. I think that gives perhaps certain hints about methods. Methods are not rules. Method is a routine. That is a difference. And I think that we really have to be honest enough that an architect starts with an image, starts with the imagination. Very often the poverty of architecture is based on the fact that we start with words, with theory, with the paper. We have to have the image in our head before putting it on paper. Therefore, I try to let people simply do the thing. People make constructions the way they see it in their heads. Moreover, it is very important that it is technically easily realizable. That means that the planning should start in their head, planning without the paper, without the drawing. The drawing is only a tool of communication. This is in a way new, but it is also thousands of years old. I am trying to present it in a way adapted to how things are today. And therefore, I see that the first step is Marcel Duchamp. The person who "used" a readymade; but before he had this idea, he had this image of the thing. However, the Merzbau is more interesting because it is not a readymade: it is randomly made.

In addition to this, again, the image is a continuous process. I am sure that Schwitters didn't see in advance what he was going to do. It developed step by step. It was a sequence, and is a pity that it couldn't be recorded as a sequence. And I think, evidently, that the city is like this: it is a process, it is not a product. Architecture is this way. Science is also that way, and so on. And now another factor comes in: the process is emotional. It is not rational. We rationalize art. And it may be that I am not right. This might give a completely different approach to architectural objects as well. There is no final state, it is a long, ongoing process. In this ongoing process everybody is participating, not only the architect.

HANS ULRICH OBRIST This leads us to what you did at the Musée d'Art moderne de la Ville de Paris, for the *Nuit Blanche* in 2003. You presented a kind of Do-It-Yourself set of instructions. You made available a lot of this white polyurethane wrapping material, and created what one could call a very fast Merzbau. It was a Merzbau that started in one night. It started empty, with a few structures you put in, and then developed some forms of very strange density, which actually led to all kinds of layers. By 3 o'clock in the morning, some graffiti artists from the Parisian suburbs appropriated your structure and painted graffiti all over. So it is no longer *about* the city, it *becomes* a city. Can you tell us a little bit about the rules or the method of this project?

YONA FRIEDMANN Let us call it Merz Action, not Merzbau Acting. My personal experience is that the most one can do is trigger a process. The process goes its own way, but you have to start it. People tell themselves it is possible, and then they go on their own. At the Biennale I was doing a project, and I just couldn't stop the workers, because they were carrying on on their own. I had a flight to catch, and they were continuing it. So there are elements in this object that I saw only later, after I had left, in a photograph. I think that this is important: to realize this kind of process.

Also, I don't talk about works of art, I talk about processes of art. We know that the public completes the work of art with its associations. I find it almost more reasonable that you make a work of art, and somebody adds something to it. From your point of view, this might be an error of aesthetics. But it is not an error from the human point of view. When I am speaking about process, I am always thinking about the human actor in it.

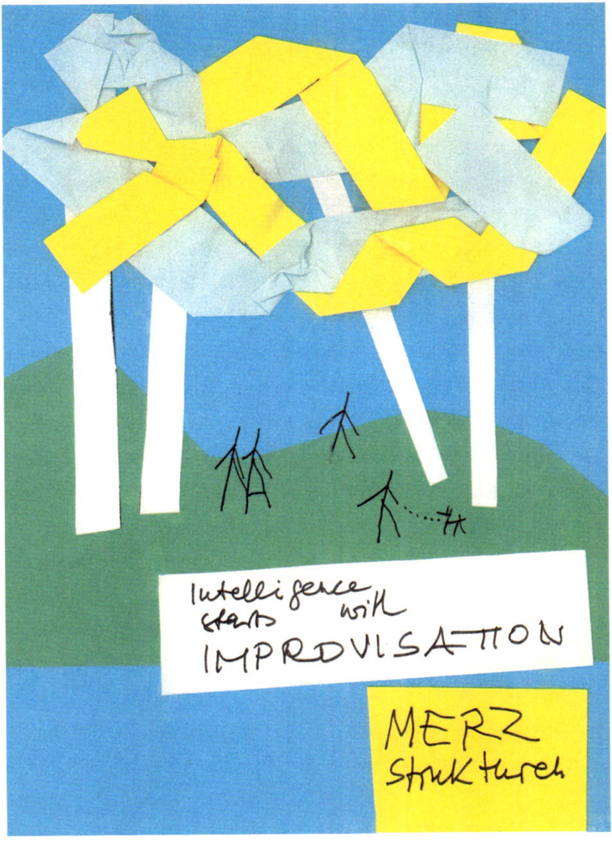

YONA FRIEDMAN *Merzstrukturer*, 2005

And this is what makes it continuous. Be it science, architecture, or whatever you want: it is not simply interaction. It is an ongoing process, an endless process. I was once saying at an architects' meeting that the building isn't finished when the architect walks off the scene. The building is finished hundreds of years later. This is even the case for demolished buildings. In Berlin, many buildings were demolished, but after the buildings had disappeared, the foundations and the property around it determined how it was rebuilt. With the World Trade Center they have been digging out the foundations for three years. All these acts are very long-lasting and that is a very different view from what we seem to have in modern architecture. However, it is true in politics. Politics are determined by hundreds of years of past history, by automatisms. We are brainwashed by history. The political process is typically such a never-ending process.

To sum up what I was saying: I was simply trying to change our way of looking at things.

HANS ULRICH OBRIST One of the things I am particularly curious to have your opinion about is this idea, which is present in many of the essays in this book and particularly strongly discussed in the one by Gwendolen Webster: the question of the Gesamtkunstwerk. Is there a danger of a totalitarizing aspect, which, as Gwendolen Webster pointed out, Dorothee Dietrich seems to reproach Schwitters' Merzbau? You have very often talked about tolerant space, the tolerant city. From your very non-totalitarian approach to architecture, how would you see the notion of the Gesamtkunstwerk now?

YONA FRIEDMANN The Gesamtkunstwerk means that the artwork is made by the public. It is really the public who create it, and it depends on the public—what they see in it and how they accept it. We cannot turn the switch and tell the public that something does not exist. In India, for example, musicians told me several times: "We play otherwise, we play differently, depending on the public. We feel the public. And the same musical piece is not the same, if we are playing to this public or to that public." The public does not participate visibly, it is only sensed. And that is really the Gesamtkunstwerk for me.

HANS ULRICH OBRIST At this point I want to bring Constant A. Nieuwenhuys into the discussion, and your exchange with him, because I think it is on this very point that there was a certain disagreement between Constant's idea of New Babylon and your idea of the city. Knowing that you had this very unique correspondence with Constant, I wanted to ask you if you could tell us a little bit about this.

YONA FRIEDMANN Constant is one of those people who make a work of art and then it is finished. But I am not looking to make a work of art; I am not able to finish it myself. It is only the public, only the user, who can finish it. I very often give a simple example. Let us take a look at social housing, a tower block 20 floors high. On every floor, the architect has drawn the same plan. However, if you enter each apartment, the arrangement is different on every floor. Because people correct and change the architect's work. And then other people come in, and it changes again. Or the same people change it.

HANS ULRICH OBRIST Another thing that is discussed in Dietmar Elgers' essay are the architectural pioneers of the early 20th century. We talked about Taut and also Finsterlin and the link of that architecture to Schwitters' Merzbau. In a recent interview done for the Tinguely Museum, Daniel Spoerri was asked about literature and the influence of the Merzbau, and it is interesting that he said that in the 1960s there was hardly any literature about the Merzbau. It was really only through firsthand sources, through people who

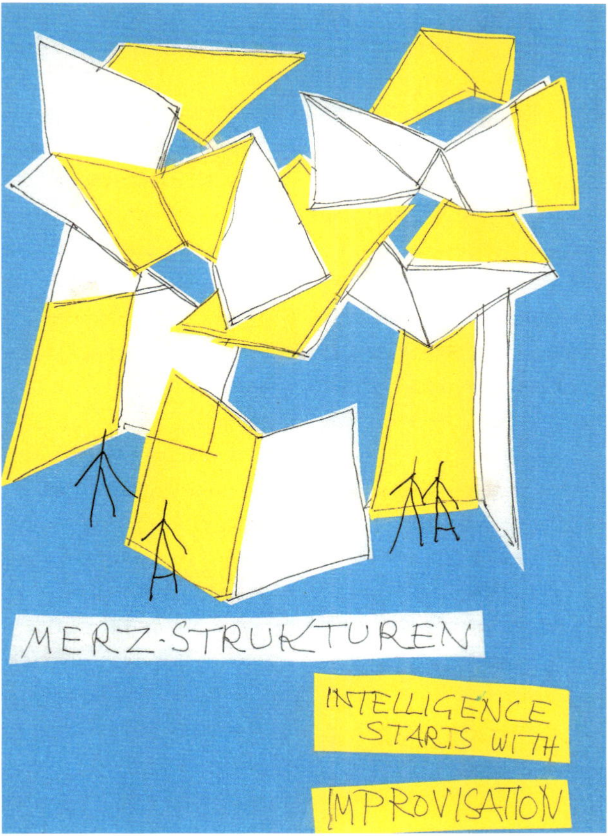

YONA FRIEDMAN *Merzstrukturen*, 2005

had actually known Schwitters, that it was possible to have access to texts. It was very complicated. A similar thing was true for all these architects like Finsterlin or Taut. There was a great degree of amnesia about many of them. Finsterlin was only rediscovered in the 1970s. Thinking about your generation of architects, I was wondering what your relationship was to these historical examples of the avant-garde of the early 20th century. Did you have access to them, or was it also more indirectly, through very scarce information, that you connected.

YONA FRIEDMANN I will give two different answers. The first is simply an anecdote. I knew Spoerri before he was starting to be an artist. One day I was with him in a café (he was with Tinguely, and we were neighbors) and in the café there were all kinds of things left on the table. And Spoerri suddenly told us: "I can glue it there, and this will be a work of art." That means I was present when he was inventing his tableau piège. I mention this only for the anecdote.

But to answer your question: when I was very young, I thought very positively about modern architecture. However, then came the Second World War—and I am practically a product of this World War, of a world were all the rules became somehow invalid. Nothing was normal and nothing was adapted to this rupture in the world. So I understood that the need, the possibility to adapt to conditions, can abruptly and brutally change. How do you live in a city where the water services are broken? How do you produce food in a city where there is no food? I found the answers in the poor neighborhoods, in the shanty towns where you have to find a way to produce your food, where you have to get your water somehow. In January 1945, I was living in a city without water, so we were drinking snow. These special conditions can happen at any moment … look at Baghdad, or the Tsunami victims on TV. A city essentially is a tool for survival. It has to be. What is survival? Again: it cannot be planned, it is improvised under pressure and it is invented by the people. People in danger become inventive.

So I think, and I don't mean it pejoratively, that all the absurdity of the Bauhaus was goodwill, too much goodwill, instead of adapting to reality. The Second World War was a lesson in reality and now we are again in a similar state. In certain periods and certain places, architecture becomes above all a status symbol. Without doubt, this is a very important element. But I think that the status symbol can also be invented by the user. In many countries people paint and decorate their houses in their own way. You saw a part of my apartment. The postman was telling me that he wished he could do the same. So I told him to just do it. And that is exactly the point: making it easy, this adaptation.

HANS ULRICH OBRIST I have a very last question. I have always been very fascinated by the fact that only a few months after Schwitters started to work on the Merzbau, Stefan Zweig wrote a very important text called *Die Monotonisierung der Welt* (*On the Monotonization of the World*, 1925), talking about globalization. Reading Stefan Zweig is almost like reading globalization critiques of today. It feels a little bit like reading Edward Glissant. One becomes aware that there have been different periods of globalization. As Glissant points out, at the moment of such homogenizing forces of globalization, as we experience it now and as Zweig seems to have experienced in 1924–1925, one possible answer to globalization in the form of resistance is through creating non-homogenized spaces. I don't think that it is by accident that the whole Merzbau discussion has come into architecture and, particularly, into the museum discussion at a moment when there is an ever increased degree of homogenization, of that sort of global branding of museum architecture. To cut a long story short, I wanted to ask you if you could tell us a little bit about your idea of globalization, about

Glissant's idea of mondialité as opposed to globalization.

YONA FRIEDMANN I use the term "mass individualism." It seems to be a contradiction, but we are living in it. Everything is homogenized and made uniform, and each of us has made an effort to break away from this and to introduce ourselves as individuals. This simply means that I have to be different from my neighbor. I think that there are very long-term examples. The most globalizing phenomenon in all human history was the incredible invention of languages, acoustic signs that are organized in a certain way. The whole thing is incredibly complex. Still, there are no two people who speak exactly the same language. Each of us has his own language. All literature is based on it: a writer is characterized by the fact that he writes differently to another. And the reader reads the same text differently to another. So this incredible globalization invention, our articulated language, is incredibly complicated. Moreover, each of us overcomplicates it in order to get his own way. The actual globalization is similar. The problem is that it is being developed too fast. It tries to impose things and this is what causes the absurdity. A slow globalization would take, say, 500 years. If it happens in 20 years, it leads to a crisis.

There is a collage on the sheet of paper floating down from the Eiffel Tower, it is an original by me. The video is called *For Reto Flury* because it pays homage to him, double homage, because for one thing it was Reto's idea to drop a newspaper page off the Eiffel Tower and let it float down, so as to follow it and watch it until one cannot see it any more—not because it has got all the way down, but because it has become absorbed into the city. We did this together two or three times while he was staying in Paris, hence the video. The other thing is, it was Reto Flury's express "last wish" that his ashes should be scattered from the Eiffel Tower, and this I did (together with his mother) after his death.

THOMAS HIRSCHHORN *For Reto Flury*, 1994, film stills

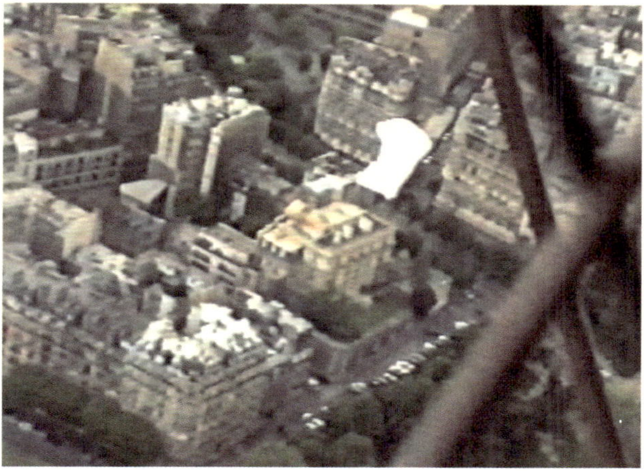

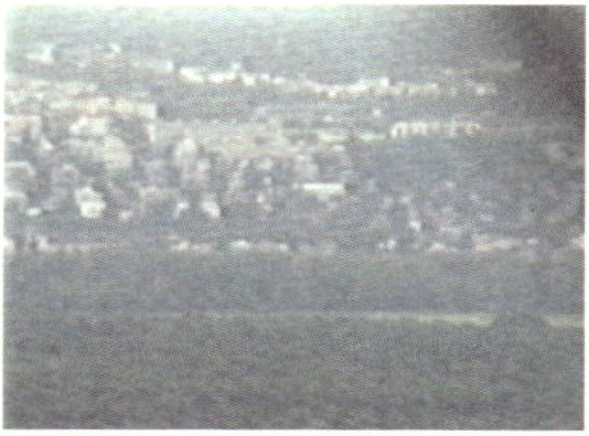

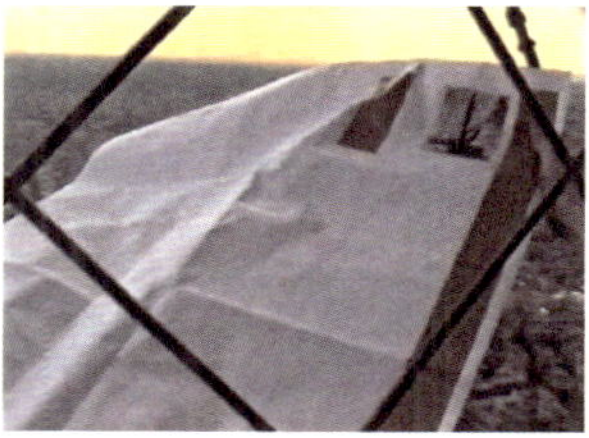

Appendix: Processing

Masami Akita aka Merzbow;
http://www.merzbow.net/

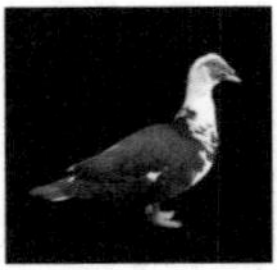

Friedman 2005
"Yona Friedman's Merzbau"
Video interview with Hans Ulrich Obrist in Yona Friedman's apartment in Paris, March 2005.

Friedman: "Many years ago, in the early 1970s, I was trying to start a movement that I called 'rubbish is beautiful,' considering that rubbish, i.e. all kinds of industrial fallout, is a raw material. It is a mine. You have mines of plastic, mines of cardboard, and no longer mines of iron or coal. I thought that the best way to transform it into something usable, is, first of all, to make a work of art out of it."

Friedman: "I believe very strongly that improvisation is the most important intellectual capacity that a human being can have. The not planned, the improvised. This means: very fast judgment, very fast action, and the right estimation of what one can do. And all of this is a program. Perhaps we might arrive at a different kind of industrial society, a development of industrial society, which could be 'the improvising society.'"

A DVD copy of this interview, 28min, English,
can be ordered at
Cabaret Voltaire
Spiegelgasse 1
CH-8001 Zurich
tel: + 41 43 268 57 20
www.cabaretvoltaire.ch
info@cabaretvoltaire.ch

Hirschhorn 2005
"Thomas Hirschhorn's Merzbau"
Video interview with Hans Ulrich Obrist in Paris, August 2005.

"A grotto is not architecture, a grotto is beyond architecture, it is nature, it is a skin, the inside of a skin. Therefore the Merzbau is not proper architecture, it is like a grotto, it is a natural phenomenon, it is an upended skin. Therefore I think it is important to know that Kurt Schwitters built the Merzbau three times, he built it over and over again around himself.

Further I want to emphasize that it is important that the Merzbau is always intended to have a person inside. Not that the person has to be interactive, but it is about the relation between the person and the ambient space. This is what interests me in the grotto. Also the grotto is a place where the person has to apply a different hierarchy, a different chronology, and a different scale."

Meyer-Büser/Orchard 2000
Aller Anfang ist Merz – Von Kurt Schwitters bis heute heute/In the Beginning Was Merz. From Kurt Schwitters to the Present Day, ed. Susanne Meyer-Büser and

Karin Orchard, exh. cat., Sprengel Museum, Hanover, Ostfildern 2000. With the following contributions:
Dietmar Elger, "Kurt Schwitters and Nouveau Réalisme," p. 296–301;
Isabell Ewig, "Father of the Fathers of Pop: Kurt Schwitters," p.290–295;
Justin Hoffmann, "'Crumple and turbulate.' Kurt Schwitters and the action art of the 1960s," p. 302–309;
Ines Katenhusen, "Kurt Schwitters und Hannover oder vom Wandel und Handel der Eingeborenen jener Siedlung, in der Herr Schwitters zu leben gezwungen ist," p. 234–243;
Ulrich Krempel, "'Atelier Merzbau'—The Merzbau in the Tradition of Artists' Studios and the Problems of its Reconstruction," p. 260–269;
Anette Kruszynski, "'My Goal is the Merzgesamtkunstwerk ... ' On the Unity Of Kurt Schwitters' Oeuvre," p. 252–259;
Susanne Meyer-Büser, "On dissapearing in Space—Walk-in Collages from Schwitters to the present day," p. 270–279;
Karin Orchard, "The Eloquence of Waste. Kurt Schwitters' Work and its Reception in America," p. 280–289;
Gerhard Schaub, "'You can't avoid Schwitters,' On the critical reception of the Merz poet since 1945," p. 310–319;
Isabel Schulz, "What would life be without Merz? On the Evolution and Meaning of Kurt Schwitters' Concept of Art," p. 244–251

Nicolin 2005

"Merzarchitektur," *Lotus,* no. 123, 2005

Essays by:

Pierluigi Nicolin, "Merzbau";

Harald Szeeman, "La tendenza all'Opera totale/The Tendency Toward the Total Work of Art";

Peter Eisenman, "L'Opera totale come sistema aperto/ The Gesamtkunstwerk as an Open System";

Anthony Vidler, "Diagrammi di utopia/Diagrams of Utopia";

Jaleh Mansoor, "Il Merzbau di Schwitters/ Kurt Schwitters' Merzbau";

Gilles Deleuze, Felix Guattar , "Bilancio-programma per macchine desideranti/Balance Program for Desiring Machines"

And featuring projects by:

Eisenman Architects; Gehry Partners; Toyo Ito & Associates; Andrea Branzi; OMA; Steven Holl Architects; Metrogramma, Alessandro Scandurra Studio; FOA; Luca Molinari; Domenico Insinga; Michael Maltzan Architecture; Boeri Studio; Juhani Pallasmaa, Rachel Whiteread and Kazuyo Sejima, Ryue Nishizawa/SANAA.

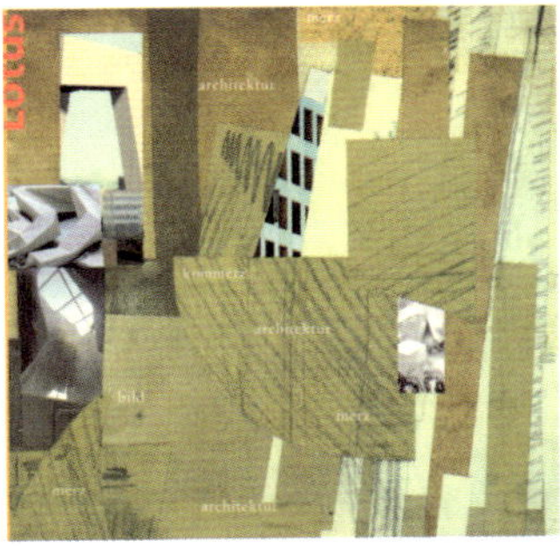

Cover of *Lotus* magazine, issue on Merzarchitektur, no. 123, 2005

Editoriale Lotus srl
Via Santa Marta 19/a
I-20123 Milan
http://www.editorialelotus.it/

Obrist 2005

"Merzspace," an essay by Hans Ulrich Obrist on artists' spaces and new forms of complexity in *spike ART QUARTERLY*, no. 04, Vienna 2005, p. 14–19.

"Pierluigi Nicolin noted that the world of architecture has recently been taking an interest in Merz architecture, and attributed this to 'the new and irresistible fascination of the incomplete ... the act of assembling a multitude of plastic forms and materials, found objects, "spoils and relics" that were enclosed and partly walled up so that they could serve as records of previous states. Incomplete on principle, growing, changing constantly ... The theme of assemblage has become a basic condition of the new globalized world ... Taken as components to be assembled rather than designed from scratch, the various frames, curtain walls, escalators, elevators, ceilings, floors, etc. and sometimes even pre-packaged models of buildings represent an archive of solutions for the designer of metropolitan megacomplexes ... composed of accidental patterns ... Lateral motion, three-dimensionality, fortuitousness ... emphasizing horizontal structures ... creating symbols of centrality rather than aiming at convergence at a point, the new Merz architecture emphasizes tangents, vanishing points, twists, and crossings, without renouncing the expression of a certain Piranesian drama in the predisposition of its new figures.'"

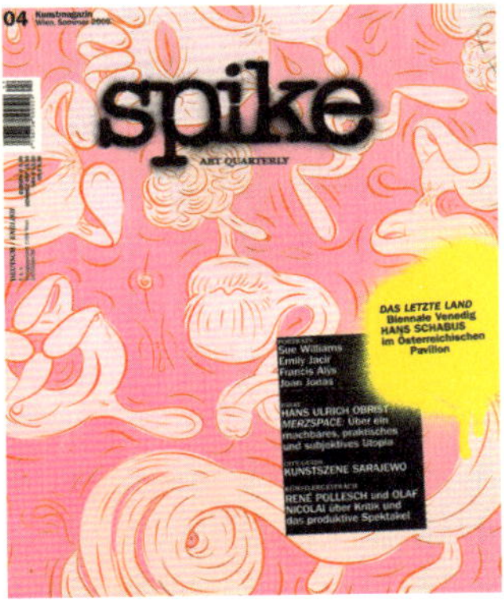

Cover of *Spike Art*, no. 04, 2005, cover image by Sue Williams, courtesy 303 Gallery New York

Sportmagazin Verlag GmbH
Heiligenstädter Lände 29
A-1190 Vienna
http://www.spikeart.at

Orozco 2005

"Gabriel Orozco's Merzbau"
Video interview with Hans Ulrich Obrist, Paris, May 2005

Gabriel Orozco: "To me, it is more about this whole enterprise of languages, which is involved in Schwitters' work. The system of his work can be transported to any media. So he can make collage, architecture, music, poetry. This system, this personal way of doing things, can be applied to various things. And it is this complexity of the system that makes the work so rich. There are many artists who are good in one medium but not many artists can create a universe that can be applied to so many disciplines."

The complete transcript of the interview carried out for the Symposium Merzbau at Cabaret Voltaire, was published in January 2006, in issue 888 of *domus*.

Domus
Editoriale Domus S.p.A.
Via G. Mazzocchi 1/3
I-20089 Rozzano Milan
http://www.domusweb.it/

This book has been published on the occasion of the Symposium Merzbau, "Historical Dimensions and Contemporary Potential" *at Cabaret Voltaire in Zurich, May 7, 2005.*

Edited by
ADRIAN NOTZ
and HANS ULRICH OBRIST

Copyediting
CLARE MANCHESTER

Design
GAVILLET & RUST/MONOD

Typeface
HERMES-SANS (WWW.OPTIMO.CH)

Cover by
YONA FRIEDMAN *Merz Stadt*, 2005

Page 1
KURT SCHWITTERS *Merzbau*, Hanover
photographed in 1933
by Wilhelm Redemann

Photo Credits
Kurt Schwitters Archive, Sprengel Museum Hanover, VG-Bild Kunst

Special thanks to
MASAMI AKITA
ZVONIMIR BAKHOTIN
CRISTINA BECHTLER
ANDRE BOURNOT
GIOVANNI CARMINE
MARC DACHY
KAREL DUDESEK
INES GEBETSROITHER
SIMON GREENBERG
MICHAEL HILTBRUNNER
DORA IMHOF
MICHAEL LOUGHRIDGE
MARIE LUSA
GUIDO MAGNAGUAGNO
PATRICK MAISANO
INGRID MECKLENBURG
PHILIPP MEIER
RAIMUND MEYER
ANJA MÜLLER-ALSBACH
MICHELLE NICOL
PIERLUIGI NICOLIN
ISABELLA DI NUNNO
GABRIEL OROZCO
ALMUT REMBGES
GREGOR SCHNEIDER
ISABEL SCHULZ
BERND SCHURER
JURI STEINER
WOLFGANG SUNDERKEMPER
ARACELY UZEDA

Printed by
CHE HUBER, Noir sur Noir, Geneva
ISBN 978-3-905701-37-1

Published by

JRP | Ringier
Letzigraben 134
CH-8047 Zurich
T +41 43 311 2750
F +41 43 311 2751
E info@jrp-ringier.com
www.jrp-ringier.com

Distribution

SWITZERLAND
Buch 2000
AVA, Verlagauslieferung AG
Centralweg 16, 8910 Affoltern a.A.
buch2000@ava.ch
www.ava.ch

FRANCE
Les Presses du réel
15 rue Quentin, F-21000 Dijon
info@lespressesdureel.com
www. lespressesdureel.com

GERMANY AND AUSTRIA
Vice Versa Vertrieb
Immanuelkirchstrasse 12
D-10405 Berlin
info@vice-versa-vertrieb.de
www.vice-versa-vertrieb.de

UK
Cornerhouse Publications
70 Oxford Street
UK-Manchester M1 5NH,
publications@cornerhouse.org
www.cornerhouse.org/books

USA
D.A.P./Distributed Art Publishers
155 Sixth Avenue, 2nd Floor
USA-New York, NY 10013
dap@dapinc.com
www.artbook.com

OTHER COUNTRIES
IDEA Books, Nieuwe Herengracht 11
NL-1011 RK Amsterdam
idea@ideabooks.nl
www. ideabooks.nl

In the same series:

BOB NICKAS
Collection Diary
English edition
ISBN 978-2-940271-68-9

CHRISTOPHE CHERIX AND JOHN TREMBLAY
Plastic
A Conversation on Vacuum-Formed Plastic Works
English edition
ISBN 978-3-905770-60-5

ELODIE PONG
We Are Knights on the Trajectories
of a Post-everything Era
French edition
ISBN 978-3-905701-36-4